# What Others Are Sayi

*"A Must Read!!! Riveting. Uplifting. A compelling hermeneutical analysis through Scriptures. This fresh interpretation is an enlightening read as hidden truths are unearth, where an examination takes place under the hood of the man, as it unveils his soul. Life changing to men. Clarification to women. Revealing to all."*

**Rev. Dr. George E. Holmes**
President Obama's National Clergy Leadership Group
Chaplain and Religious Chair of the DC Democratic State Committee

*"With unbending fortitude, John Guns has created an informative and inspirational book for Black men of all ages. He reminds us of our Godly-ordained role as strong and powerful men of God."*

**Rev. Dr. Charles E. Booth, Senior Pastor**
Mt. Olivet Baptist Church, Columbus, OH

*"The writing is crisp, clear, and colorful. The messages in this book speaks boldly to the issues that are facing our community."*

**Rev. Dr. Calvin Matthews, Senior Pastor**
Isle of Patmos Baptist Church, Washington, DC

*"A profoundly important collection of sermons that will help men understand their power and purpose. I promise you this book will bless you beyond your imagination."*

**Rev. Dr. Sir Walter Mack, Senior Pastor**
Union Baptist Church, Winston-Salem, NC

*"An exceptionally important book for the uplifting of Black men."*
**Rev. Dr. D. Darrell Griffin, Senior Pastor**
Oakdale Covenant Church, Chicago, IL

# The SOUL
## OF MANHOOD

**Messages to Restore, Reclaim, and Refocus the African American Male**

COMPILED BY JOHN E. GUNS
FOREWORD BY LEONARD N. SMITH

Published by MMGI Books, Chicago, IL 60636

www.mmgibooks.com

The Soul of Manhood: Messages to Restore, Reclaim, and Refocus the African American Male

Except for quotations from Scripture, the quoted ideas expressed in the book are not, in all cases, exact quotations, as some have been edited for clarity and brevity. In all cases, the author has attempted to maintain the speaker's original intent. In some cases, quoted material for this book was obtained from secondary sources, primarily print media. While every effort was made to ensure the accuracy of these sources, the accuracy cannot be guaranteed. For additions, deletions, corrections, or classifications in future editions of this text, please write Manuscript Management Group, Inc.

Scriptures marked NIV are from the Holy Bible, New International Version, Copyright © 1973, 1978, 1984 by International Bible Society. Used by permission of Zondervan Publishing House. All rights reserved.

Scriptures by NKJV are taken from the New King James Version. Copyright © 1982 by Thomas Nelson, Inc. Used by permission. All rights reserved.

Scriptures marked NLT are taken from the Holy Bible, New Living Translation, copyright © 1996. Used by permission of Tyndale House Publisher's, Inc. Wheaton, Illinois 60189. All rights reserved.

Scriptures marked KJV are taken from the King James Version.

Library of Congress Cataloging-in-Publication Data

The Soul of Manhood: Messages to Restore, Reclaim, and Refocus the African American Male

p. cm

ISBN 978-1-939774-17-0 (pbk. :alk. Paper)

Religious life. 2. Men – Conduct of life. 3. Christian – Development. MMGI BOOKS

Printed in the U.S.A.

# Foreword

*Leonard N. Smith*

**On April 30, 1930**, Columbia records released a Gospel/Blues single by Blind Willie Johnson entitled "The Soul of a Man." The song opens with the following lyrics:

> *"Won't somebody tell me*
> *Answer if you can!*
> *I want somebody to tell me*
> *Just what is the soul of a man?"*

The lyrics are the poetic expression of a thought-provoking inquiry. This is clearly a philosophical question, yet it spiritually demands an answer. Such a question not only queries one's intellect, but it also prompts an intense introspective examination if taken seriously. This is certainly not a new question. It is a haunting reminder of the spiritual quest of all humanity.

Let's briefly consider the imagery of the man behind the lyrics, which has nothing to do with Blind Willie Johnson, but has everything to do with an ordinary African American man during the 1930s.

This song conveys what I'd consider the obvious struggle of such a man during the height of the Depression. As if his quest for economic stability weren't enough, the singer's ultimate quest is to discern the soul of a man.

So, just what is a man's soul?

While the sacred Scriptures clearly convey what a man is, they vaguely reveal what a soul is. What is clear is that the soul is a critical component of our human nature. Biblically, we are viewed as a tremendous trichotomy; we are body, soul, and spirit:

May the God who gives us peace make you holy in every way and keep your whole being—spirit, soul, and body—free from every fault at the coming of our Lord Jesus Christ. (1 Thessalonians 5:23, GNT

The word of God is alive and active, sharper than any double-edged sword. It cuts all the way through, to where soul and spirit meet, to where joints and marrow come together. It judges the desires and thoughts of the heart. (Hebrews 4:12, GNT)

The body is the part of a man that people see. The spirit is that part that people want to know. The "soul" of a man is that part that can never be fully known, not even by the man himself. A man can communicate what's in his body and convey what's in his spirit but can never articulate what's in his soul.

While I believe that we are all three, and the above Scriptures affirm this belief, there are those who have challenged and changed this supposition. Some have suggested that we are a dichotomy instead of a trichotomy, to the extent that it is a time-honored theological debate. The proof of my assertion is seen in the fact that many Christians use soul and spirit interchangeably. However, the two are not one in the same.

A man's "spirit" is where both his faith and hope abide, and is also the scared place where he reverences, worships, and prays to God. The "soul" of a man is the residence of his affections, creativity, consciousness, memory, and thoughts. It is his immaterial, invisible, and immortal self, the very seat of his emotions, mind, and will.

The soul of a man is the treasure trove of his trust and repository of his reminiscences. His soul is where a man abates his agony, confronts his challenges, faces his flaws, harbors his hurts, and designs his decisions.

A man's soul is literally the silo of his unpretentious human self, where the crown jewel of God's creation, without fear, rendezvous with the painful memories of the past of both he and his ancestors, but has the awesome privilege of previewing the Godly potential of them all. It is the clandestine compartment where he bears his burdens, without having to prove that he is a man because he is reminded that he is by the very God who created him.

You can never see into a man's soul, but you can see into the soul of his manhood.

In the soul of an African American man's manhood, you will discover how he sees himself as a man, how he defines manhood, his silent struggles to be a man, and the unreasonable demands for him to be the man of someone else's dreams.

To understand an African American man, you must first understand his perception of manhood and most assuredly, the unreasonable demands placed upon him to be regarded as a man. While the demands are reasonable by most accounts, when the demands shift with the mood of the demander, it's hard to be consistently seen as a man.

One of the many unreasonable demands, which constantly confront an African American male, is the necessity to prove that he is a real man. (While this may seem inconsequential, it really isn't!) This culturally infused compulsion is undergirded by his instinctive impulse to demonstrate his manhood. This often results in behaviors that are deemed socially inappropriate or generally unnecessary. As a result of how he sees manhood grossly differing from what others demand of him, he then becomes confused and believes that negatively standing out translates into standing up and being a man. This, coupled with the unexplainable insatiable appetite that some women have for "bad boys," fuels his need to be noticed and affirmed as a man – often without justly considering the nonsensicality of the demands or the consequences of his behavior. This places the proof of his manhood exclusively in his own hands.

In a man's soul, he is a man! Therefore, he never has to prove that he is what God designed him to be. This is because in his soul, he is stripped by God of his control, taken into the control of the Holy Spirit, yet never fears being out of control!

Since you can never know what's in the soul of a man, this book will guide you on an exclusive scripted expedition into the surreptitious substance of the soul of manhood!

# Table of Contents

# Restore...

***Restore*** is to cause something or someone to be returned to its original condition – its intended use; or to place something or someone back where it belongs. Black men must assume an active role in the process of being restored to their divine placement as sons and servants to and of God.

It is easy to understand the meaning of *Restore* when it applies to things like vintage cars and antique furniture. People who restore old cars have a passion for returning these cars to their original condition; there is an excitement in the owners when they are able to display the finished product – a gleaming paint job, power under the hood, overhauled brake systems and more. The connection can be made between the wear and tear, the hard work required, and the expense of time and money to make cars and furniture new again. But how easy is it to actually *restore* something or someone without an intentional and deliberate will to do so—especially if that someone is you?

The truth is, to *Restore* – more often than not – is very hard, but not impossible, to do. In some cases, it is even hard to acknowledge that one needs to be restored. For example, take the hard-working and driven person whose physical body needs to be restored from mental and physical fatigue; many can see the need to be restored except that person. As well, a most prevalent example of delayed acknowledgement is when trust has been betrayed and faith must be restored. The hard work of restoring the betrayer back to a place of integrity and the betrayed back to a level of unconditional trust begins with acknowledging the need and desire to be restored.

To engage a process of restoring your public life and private life means to unleash the power that God has placed within you to put things in their intended order. God is the great Restorer or people, places, and things and provides evidence in Scripture that support how important it is to restore or be restored. At least thirty-nine references to the word restore appear in the King James Version of the Bible. They include:

- 1 Thessalonians 5:23 that assures a man will be restored and have peace when his *"whole spirit and soul and body [is kept] blameless unto our Lord Jesus Christ."*

- Ps. 51:12 in which David cries out *"Restore unto me the joy of thy salvation..."* David acknowledges that his joy was lost and needs to be restored.

- Jeremiah 30 assures us that God will restore the people, and

- Galatians 6:1 that encourages us to restore others *"in the spirit of meekness…"*

ALL MEN need at some point to be restored to God. Restoration strengthens man's inner being, and strengthens his soul. Why do we need to be restored to God? Many of us have allowed our hearts to be taken from our creator. Therefore, we must allow the Spirit to God to help redirect our hearts and paths back to the will of God. It is man's obligation to work to restore His soul to God as the soul of man belongs to God.

In the restoration process, we seek God to mend the schisms that are in our souls, the fractures and cracks that the enemy has used to slip in and work to destroy our relationships with God, the church and family. Nobody is exempt from the wiles of the enemy. Therefore, we all are in the much needed position for restoration. In Ephesians, we are reminded of the contrary walk we have participated in as mere humans. Whether we blatantly committed an act contrary to God's Word or was a passive participant or an accessory, the act worked to separate us from God. Once again Paul reminds us in the Word that we all have been participants in wrongdoing, but God is standing ready to restore us to Him. Paul writes in Ephesians,

> *"Wherein in time past ye walked according to the course of this world, according to the prince of the power of the air, the spirit that now worketh in the children of disobedience. Among whom also we all had our conversation in times past in the lusts of our flesh, fulfilling the desires of the flesh and of the mind; and were by nature the children of wrath, even as others. But God…"* (Ephesians 2:2-4).

It is the latter phrase, "But God" that allows us to be restored to Him. It is the love and mercy of God that allow fallen mankind to be restored. God wants to heal the broken and contrite spirit. Praise God for restoration!

The sermons in this book give insight, inspiration, and impetus for the reader to allow his soul to be *Restored* to the purpose(s) and will of God. Whether encompassed by your spiritual madness or engulfed in your pain, the process to *Restore* is there for you.

# Dealing with My Spiritual Madness

*Timothy M. Rainey II*

Mark 5:1-20

*We* all have the potential to experience madness. During the dark moments of life when a man's soul is possessed by vexing emotions and moods that quiet the voice of God, it is arguable that that man has entered into a state of spiritual madness. A man is subject to such madness whenever he finds that his life is possessed or controlled by feelings like anger, depression, or disappointment more than he is guided by his spiritual intuitions. We find the demoniac of Gadara1 victimized by such possession in the fifth chapter of Mark's Gospel. The circumstances of his life cause him to fall prey to foreign spirits and the impact of their possession over him is so menacing that the man not only regresses to a state of madness but in his madness he is driven to wailing desperately in the hillsides, lonely and living among the dead. How tragic. How painful. Madness is not a distant possibility for any human soul birthed into this uncertain world of ours. A moment of candor would reveal that some of us are no more than one heartbreak, one tragedy, one misfortunate experience away from spiritual madness in our own lives. And there are others of us who would have to admit that we exist in a state of madness right now.

In this book, there are many rich biblical texts used to help black males become better men; it is my prayer that you read the demoniac's story as one of those texts and that it releases you from whatever binds your spiritual thriving. If black men are to maintain peace of mind in light of the evils of this world, we must first acknowledge that spiritual madness as a very real and present threat. To deal with these evils we must also become increasingly aware that finding peace in our own lives, just as in the case of the demoniac, requires nothing less than a genuine encounter with the Christ.

## Madness and the Demoniac

The account of the demoniac has all the qualities of good cinema. In it there is drama, desperation, suspense, and of course, redemption. During a difficult period in this man's life he becomes possessed by not one but an entire legion of demon spirits,[2] spirits that come to exist in him so long that they assume their own identity within his body. Possession keeps a man from feeling like himself. In this state one's emotions begin to take on

5

their own life of bitterness, anger, resentment, and fear. For the demoniac these moments are so dark and lonely that his madness renders him unfit to live among civilization and he is ultimately driven to reside among the graves of men and women long gone from this earth. The piercing shrill of his wailing travels from the distant hills and reaches the city streets. And what is even more painful are the images painted by the Gospel writer of the brutal, self-inflicted tortures he makes upon his own body. He is truly a man possessed.

Whenever I revisit this story I find myself empathetically engaged in this narrative because I too have struggled through times of deep possession. In my life I have experienced times of bitter lovelessness. In my attempt to exude an image of strength, invulnerability, and a life ruled by dispassionate logic, I began to empty myself of the capacity to feel anything intimate for anyone. I was no longer the compassionate and sensitive person I had always been. It didn't take long for me to end up just like the man we find in the fifth chapter of Mark. My spirit was defiled, my soul raged out of control, my cruel behaviors could not be bound and in the midnight of my experience. I found few moments of rest because even in sleep my emotions rioted agonizingly in the dead places of my own spiritual decay.

To be sure there have been times when I have been possessed by the spirit of lovelessness. And while I do have empathy with the demoniac on the point of possession I must move quickly to arrive at how profoundly I identify with his moment of healing. What this story also reveals to me is that even in the utter chaos and stormy night of our possession there is peace to be found just at the shore of where our madness meets the Savior. This story is full of rich imagery and metaphors and we must no fail to see how brilliantly it speaks wisdom, power, and authority into our lives, even today.

### Madness and the Spirituality of Black Men

Black men must recognize the importance of spiritual healthiness. I have to speak to brothers candidly here because we have too often overlooked this area of our living. To find evidence of how men as a whole neglect spiritual matters we need not look any further than the disproportionate ratio of women to men in the black church. Researchers on the African American church have found that men make up only approximately 30 percent of black congregations; which means that for every three black women in church on Sunday morning, there is only one man.[3] The factors that play into this disparaging ratio surely range in number and are deeply complex, but here I am primarily concerned with the theory (though a generalized one) that men are most often unreceptive to church that is characterized (rightly or wrongly) with femininity. I often hear brothers express a non-desire for worship services that attempt to coax them into elaborate emotional expressions and a spirituality of inner intimacy. And while certain aspects of church do in fact call us to think and act in ways that are stereotypically non-masculine, men must learn to engage their spiritual selves in spite of this these flawed portrayals.

A man's spirit is a real and functional component of his living. It grows with him, produces tangible effects in a man's life, and just as a bodily organ it too can get out of whack. Such spiritual disorder proves to be a reality in the case of the demoniac whose affliction was given the ancient diagnosis – demon possession. Today demon possession does not hold the relevance it once did in biblical times, but once this ancient malady is nuanced and reconsidered, we'll find that this text provides Bible readers with a wealth of insight on the intersecting worlds of soul and psyche.

When demon possession is alluded to in the Scriptures, this condition is generally understood, by psychological-critical interpreters of the Bible, as the condition of persons who suffer from physical or psychical disorders that work to subjugate the personality of the afflicted person. Wayne G. Rollins, in his book *Soul & Psyche: The Bible in Psychological Perspective*, invokes the work of a renowned author in biblical psychology when he writes, "All agree that the so-called demon-possessed are suffering from multiple personality disorder or, as Wise put it, are 'persons in who destructive energies have overcome creative energies, whose life and energies are not organized and directed toward satisfying goals.'"[4] Everybody's story is different, but I'm willing to wager that destructive energies are always at the foundation of spiritual possession. Destructive energies are those things that strip the joy, love, and happiness from our lives. Such things depress us and weaken our morals and ethics. And if readers of the Gospel are to gain inspiration from this text that moves us toward possessing productive energies, we must not simply perceive this man and marvel at his incredible outrage but we must attempt to understand his anger and anguish and discover each painful reality that might indeed be true of ourselves.

So the question for us today is what happens in possession that would allow for us to feel as if we are not ourselves or as if something has overtaken us? I've discovered in my own life that possession has more to do with how our Christian sensibilities deteriorate rather than how foreign spirits overcome us. When we are possessed it is because our humanity has been reduced to a lower level of existence. A man plunges to inferior levels of living whenever the Christian gifts of the spirit – love, joy, peace, longsuffering, kindness, goodness, faithfulness, gentleness, self-control[5] – are neglected within that life. These are qualities that are not only peculiar to the Christian life but to any person in pursuit of the highest standard of living. But when the Christian man is no longer obedient to these qualities he becomes lost and misdirected, he moves about in a frenzy, his mind and emotions rage from morning 'til night, and we are in many ways brought down to the level of basic animality. In his brilliant work Madness and Civilization, Michel Foucault writes:

> The animality that rages in madness dispossesses man of what is specifically human in him; not in order to deliver him over to other powers, but simply to establish him at the zero degree of his own nature. For classicism, madness in its ultimate form is man in immediate relation to his animality, without other reference, without any recourse.[6]

In the demoniac we are given evidence of such animalism through the wildness of his behavior, the breaking loose of chains and wailing deep into the night. But even more than this physical unrest it is his spiritual wildness giving way to that unrest that truly concerns me. We must remember that it was not a doctor or psychiatrist who healed the demoniac; rather, it was the Gospel made flesh, the Word Incarnate himself, Jesus Christ. So, if clinical madness is concerned with the loss of human sensibilities, spiritual madness is then the result of losing our religious sensibilities.

Our reality may not be *possession* by demonic spirits but perhaps we experience *possession* by insecurity, envy, lies, infidelity, unhappiness, guilt, opportunism, and undignified ambitiousness. And these are all things that can strip us of the spiritual fruits we might normally possess. The loss of spiritual things is what causes us to destroy friendships, mistreat the women we love, ruin our integrity, and neglect our need of Christ's Gospel and Salvation. So, when I speak of spiritual madness in the 21st century, I'm concerned with how the fruits of a Christian spirit become disintegrated and fragmented so that we are no longer obedient to what Christ's Gospel commands of us. Spiritual madness is concerned with how moods and emotions throw our lives into chaos, leaving our souls devoured and in desperate need of a recovered Christian sensibility.

Gaining a better awareness of our spiritual health is particularly critical for the African American male. When I consider our disturbing past and all the residual effects of our history in this country, one that is wrought with racism and hate toward black people and black masculinity, the state of my sanity feels less permanent than uncertain. I find it imperative that we embrace the abundance of love the Bible teaches us through the person of Christ. The dejection we feel as a result of racism can drive us to hate, fear, and defeat – all moods and emotions that can potentially possess us.

To be sure, African Americans have dealt with a long history of tragic experiences. The Middle Passage, chattel slavery, Jim Crow, and racism are all experiences that have worked to empty black bodies of all the hope, liveliness, joy, compassion, and love that a human spirit could possibly embody. In his essay *"Lord of the Crucified,"* Matthew V. Johnson explains that slavery was so successful in its mission to degrade the humanity of black people that its systematic "breaking down" of people transcended the weakening of mind and body to ultimately penetrate and disintegrate the soul. Johnson uses the term *sparagmos*, which is Greek for ritual death or dismemberment, to illustrate this tragic worldview. He expounds on this consideration by noting that:

> This syndrome created a stressed field of being in which African Americans were threatened with psychic fragmentation. The fact that African Americans were torn away from their own land and culture and unable to settle in the one where they were physically located institutionalized their marginalization as a group along with threats of separation, loss of control over bodily integrity, daily brutality, chronic mourning, and all the other factors that configured the institutionalized terror of slavery, creating and sustaining a traumatic field in which African American Christian and cultural consciousness emerged. There was a permanent sense of homelessness in what it meant to be African American. In some way, then, African Americans never fully emerged from the Middle Passage: they remain still very much on the water, struggling with titanic forces that threaten their spiritual integrity.[7]

Here, Johnson gives us a concise commentary on the spiritual tortures that black folk have had to endure throughout history. This abuse has been the result of families being stripped from the land wherein their histories, ancestry, and spiritual roots are located. He argues that these psychical tortures became so foundational to the way in which African Americans came to construct their sense of identity in this country that even though we are now decades removed from the institution of slavery part of our identities still remain connected to a culture of victimization. It is this culture of victimization and tragedy, Johnson claims, that provides for a peculiar connection between black folk and the crucified Lord.

Still, Johnson goes on to say, in our religion we must not establish such a romantic ideal of that connection that we sustain our role as victims. His conclusion has particular relevance for black men who have often suspected the church of being too docile and victimized in the face of social and political oppression (a.k.a. Martin Luther King, Jr. and nonviolent resistance) and therefore attempt to combat social evils such as racism with aggression and audacity alone, at times doing so without our faith's spiritual gifts, the most critical of which is love. I appreciate this story of the demoniac because for all of its strangeness and peculiarity it leads us directly in the path of God's saving power and puts us back in touch with the greatest baron of love this world has ever known, Jesus Christ.

### Madness and the Salvation of Black Men

Any time I read a text, I never leave that work of Scripture without searching for the imperative it provides me. I always want to know, What is God's Word compelling me to do? I look at the characters in a story and the people who interacted with Christ. I attempt to learn from their mistakes and grow by committing myself to studying the good they accomplished and doing those things in my own life. But this is a text I struggle with when engaged in that endeavor because as I think about the maddened condition of this man, it seems that he was not in a position to do much of anything on his own. I would love to be able to say that he ran to Jesus even in his madness and worshipped the Savior, that amidst his raving wildness he had a singular moment of lucidity where he recognized the power of the Savior and submitted to him. But the truth is that the demoniac was so possessed that we don't even see his character until the end of the story, after Christ has exorcised the demons that stood between his captive existence the life he was unable to live for himself. When he ran to Jesus it was under the compulsion of the spirits possessing him, and the only reason they went to Jesus was to parlay some degree of mercy from the master whom they knew could destroy them at will. So, while I know that whenever I encounter the Christ, he will reach out to me and heal me, I'm left with trying to understand what role I'm called to play during the times I feel powerless to deal with the problems that afflict me.

We can't know very much about what was going on in the spirit and mind of this man, but one thing that is certain is that until the moment he encountered the Savior, if he did nothing else, we know that he survived.

What is interesting is that the same legion of demons that entered the pigs and immediately killed them were the same demons that took over the man but was yet unable to destroy him.

So much in this world threatens to break down and destroy the spiritual being that we all are. God surely meets us where we are to love, lift, and save us at times when we could do none of these things for ourselves. And in those moments we are challenged to simply hold on until Christ meets us at the shores of our madness. And when He's done with us, the next time the world sees us, we'll be clothed and in our right mind.

> *I will extol You, O LORD, for You have lifted me up,*
> *And have not let my foes rejoice over me.*
> *O LORD my God, I cried out to You,*
> *And You healed me.*
> *O LORD, You brought my soul up from the grave;*
> *You have kept me alive, that I should not go down to the*
> *pit.*
>
> *Sing praise to the LORD, You saints of His,*
> *And give thanks at the remembrance of His holy name.*
> *For His anger is but for a moment,*
> *His favor is for life;*
> *Weeping may endure for a night,*
> *But joy comes in the morning.* (Psalm 30:1-5, NKJV)

## Notes

1. While biblical historians suggests a number of potential locations for the actual setting of this story, such as Gerasenes and Gerasa, commentators on the Synoptic Gospels generally agree that Gadara is a better fit for the location of the text and is within reasonable proximity to the Galilean shore where Jesus would have docked; James Luther Mays, ed., Interpretation: A Bible Commentary for Teaching and Preaching, Luke by Fred B. Craddock (Louisville: John Knoxville Press, 1990), 116.
2. A legion in the Roman army was 5,000 men. Bible interpreters suspect that this narrative must have had some political meaning for the Jewish readers who were subjects of the Roman Empire during this time. This "legion" being conquered by Jesus and cast into a herd of pigs that ultimately ran to their death surely spoke hope and power into the lives of many; Patrick D. Miller, David L. Bartlett eds., Westminster Bible Companion, Mark, by Douglas R.A. Hare (Louisville: Westminster John Knox Press, 1996), 65.
3. C. Eric Lincoln, and Lawrence H. Mamiya, The Black Church in the African American Experience (London: Duke University Press, 2003), 304.
4. Wayne G. Rollins, Soul and Psyche: The Bible in Psychological Perspective (Minneapolis: Fortress Press, 1999), 135.
5. Galatians 5:22-23, NKJV.
6. Michel Foucault, Madness and Civilization: A History of Insanity in the Age of Reason (New York: Random House, Inc., 1965; reprint, New York: Vintage Books, 1988), 74.
7. Matthew V. Johnson, "Lord of the Crucified" in The Passion of the Lord: African American Reflections, James A Noel and Matthew V. Johnson, eds. (Minneapolis: Fortress Press, 2005), 12-13.

# Overcoming the Mancession

*Daniel Corrie Shull*
Mark 10:46-52

*During* the global financial crisis of 2008 and the subsequent economic downturn dubbed "The Great Recession," economists and social theorists noticed an alarming trend as it related to the casualties of the recession. As data was compiled and analyzed concerning the recession it was revealed that the greatest impact of the economic downturn was felt by men. The unemployment rate of men was 50% higher than that of their female counterparts. Consequently, cultural commentators and economists gave this recession a nickname; they called it "The Mancession." The majority of jobs lost as a consequence of the recession were jobs held predominantly by men in the manufacturing and construction industries. The simple fact was that when things stopped being built, men were displaced from the economy.

Cultural and economic change always reinforce one another; therefore when nothing was being constructed and disproportionate numbers of men lost their jobs, the effects began to be felt throughout the culture. Family therapists have long pointed out that men who lose their ability to contribute financially to their family often suffer with a diminished sense of self-worth, which often leads to the withdrawal from their families, the dissolution of their marriages and intimate relationships, and in some cases total emotional and social shutdown. This is what inspired Hanna Rosin, a journalist for the Atlantic, to write her controversial yet groundbreaking essay that she entitled, "The End of Men," in which she chronicled the social changes and role reversals that are occurring globally in response to post-industrial economic realities. While millions of intelligent women are earning graduate and post-graduate degrees in the most prestigious universities, ever-increasing numbers of men—especially African American and Latino men—are becoming casualties of the prison industrial complex. As innovative women are moving into top-tier leadership in government, corporate America, and in most other places within society, it is becoming more and more prevalent for men to be marked absent in the leadership of their homes and communities of faith. In public schools across this nation our daughters in many cases are thriving and excelling while, in too many instances, our sons are failing miserably.

When all things are considered – economics, educational achievement, social engagement, familial commitment – it seems that the mancession extends far beyond the economic realities of the day. While the economic and educational gains of women should be celebrated, encouraged, and supported, the mancession – the withdrawal of men from our churches, our homes, and our communities – and men's well-being ought to concern us particularly because God has created the world in such a way that requires mutual contributions. This means that women have something critical to give and men have something critical to give and when either men or women are unable to maximize their potential and operate at their optimum capacity we are all the poorer.

It's not an either/or, it's a both/and! Every man wants a woman who has both substance and soul, and every woman wants a man who has something to bring to the table. Therefore, overcoming the mancession is critical to the health and the flourishing of our society because if half of the society is regressing, the whole of society will suffer. Overcoming the mancession economically demands that men apply themselves more rigorously in education to become marketable in growing industries such as technology. Overcoming the mancession socially demands that men develop skills in the arena of emotional intelligence and empathy and 21st-century modes of leadership.

Just as the global economy is recovering from the recession, the mancession can be overcome. In fact, as a Christian I can't help but look at life through the lenses of a theological perspective that says "with God all things are possible." No matter how long you've been down you can get back up. You may be sidelined but God can realign. Your resources may be dwindling but God still is very capable of providing "all of your needs according to his riches in glory." Maybe certain areas of your life have been shut down but I've got good news: The windows of Heaven are still wide open! Recessions don't last forever and mancessions can be overcome!

The tenth chapter of the Gospel of Mark chronicles the crisis of a brothah who had been sidelined because of his lack of sight. His name was Bartimaeus. He was the son of Timaeus, and as was customary he sat alongside of the main thoroughfare in Jericho to beg for benevolence from pilgrims passing through. But the scene shifts in verse 47, when Mark intriguingly notes that this blind beggar heard that Jesus was passing by.

We ought not run over that too quickly. This blind beggar heard that Jesus was passing by, which means that this man positioned himself in such a way as to maximize what he had left.

And it is here that we extract the first lesson as it relates to overcoming the mancession: **We must learn to maximize what we have left.** Bartimaeus did not have sight but he did have ears and he used his ears to compensate for the sight that he lacked. And that's a critical principle for anyone who hopes to overcome anything: maximize what you have! God always leaves you with something. You may be down to your last dime but a dime plus God will do things that a million dollars without God can never accomplish. God never gives anybody everything but he gives everybody something; you've just got to maximize the something that you've got! What skill, what resource, what connection, what tool, what gift do you have? And how are you maximizing it to get what you need to get and go where you need to go? Maximize what you have left! That's what Bartimaeus did! He positioned himself in such a way that he could take full advantage of the resource that he did have – his hearing, despite his lack of sight.

Mark says that Bartimaeus heard that Jesus was passing by, and when he heard that he must have been reminded of the other stuff that he overheard as people were passing by or talking in the vicinity about Jesus. He remembered overhearing how Jesus healed the woman with the issue of blood. He remembered overhearing how Jesus restored sight to the blind man just a little piece down the road. He remembered overhearing how Jesus just spoke a word and the centurion's servant was healed. He remembered overhearing about the lepers whom Jesus had made clean. And when he remembered all that he had overheard he knew that this was the moment wherein he could overcome what had overcome him. He was blind so he didn't know what Jesus looked like; he couldn't walk up to Jesus and touch his garment like the woman with the issue of blood, so he did the best that he could do – he lifted up his voice and cried out, "Jesus, son of David, have mercy on me!"

Here Bartimaeus gives us another lesson about overcoming the mancession, or anything else that you need to overcome: **Pray bold prayers!** "Jesus, son of David, have mercy on me!" Bartimaeus knew the right name to call. He knew the right person to address. He knew the one who could hook him up was in the vicinity and he had the wherewithal to call his name! There is power in the name of Jesus! Angels start moving at the name of Jesus! Demons start trembling at the name of Jesus! There is restoration in the name of Jesus! There is healing at the name of Jesus! Philippians 2 verse 9 says: "God has highly exalted him and given him a name that is above every name, that at the name of Jesus every knee shall bow and every tongue shall confess that Jesus Christ is Lord to the glory of God the Father!" There is power in that name! If you're in trouble, call that name. If you need a way out, call that name! If you need a way over, call that name! If you can't see your way through, call that name!

That's what Bartimaeus did! "Jesus, son of David, have mercy on me!" Oftentimes, people pray in whispered voices and hushed tones, but not Bartimaeus! His prayer was the loudest prayer recorded in Scripture! Bartimaeus's voice soared above the crowd, called Jesus' name, identified him as Messiah, and petitioned him to be merciful! And like Bartimaeus, when we go to God we ought to go to God with passion and stamina and confidence that He will hear us and answer our prayer!

There, of course, were people there who tried to shut Bartimaeus up. Hush up, Bartimaeus! He doesn't have time for you, Bartimaeus! He's on his way somewhere, Bartimaeus. You're embarrassing yourself, Bartimaeus. Bartimaeus, shut up! But Mark says old Bart got louder! He cried all the more: "JESUS, SON OF DAVID, HAVE MERCY ON ME!"

Bartimaeus was not deterred by the people who were attempting to hush him up; he kept calling Jesus until he got an answer! Bartimaeus wholeheartedly pursued Jesus by the only means available to him. And it's here that Bartimaeus teaches us the third principle about overcoming the mancession or whatever it is that you need to overcome: **Passionately pursue the desire of your heart even if that means risking ridicule.**

Now I'm sure that there were other blind beggars sitting around the same place where Bartimaeus was because that was the custom of the day. All people who were unable to provide for themselves as a consequence of being marginalized sat along that same route. But nobody else was hollering. The difference between Bartimaeus and the rest of the blind and lame and deaf people around him was that Bartimaeus decided that blindness and begging was not his destiny! That's why he risked ridicule. That's why he was so passionate. Bartimaeus wasn't concerned about what anybody thought of him. He needed a blessing from Jesus and he did what he had to do until he got it! And sometimes in this life you've got to do what you've got to do! You can't be concerned about what anybody else thinks; you just got to do you! You've got to "keep your eyes on the prize and hold on!" Forget public opinion. Forget fitting in with crowd. Forget faking it until you make it! I've got to passionately pursue what I'm after even if other folk don't understand!

As a consequence of Bartimaeus's passion, Jesus stopped in his tracks and instructed his disciples to call Bartimaeus. And when the disciples called Bartimaeus, they said, "Take heart! Get up! He's calling you!" That's God's word for some Brotha reading this sermon on today: "Take heart! Get up! He's calling you!" You've had some bad breaks but: "Take heart! Get up! He's calling you!" You've been on the sidelines for too long now: "Take heart! Get up! He's calling you!" The divorce is final, the foreclosure is done, the business venture failed, that relationship didn't exactly work out, that decision was not your best decision, it is what it is; "Take heart! Get up! He's calling you!"

Take heart; stop feeling sorry for yourself. If nobody else encourages you, encourage yourself! Get up! Stop wasting your life. Stop crying woe is me. You can't drink away your disappointment. You can't smoke away your pain. You can't sex away the memory of that failure. GET UP! He's calling you – to become more than what you've ever been, to try new feats, to conquer your failures, to lead your family, to care for your children, to be present and participatory!

Take heart! Get up! He's calling you! That's what the disciples said to Bartimaeus. And when Bartimaeus heard those words he threw off his cloak and sprung up to see Jesus! When you discover that God isn't through with you, that your best days are not behind you but ahead of you, your first response ought to be to throw off anything and everything that stands in between you and Jesus. "Lay aside every weight and the sin which doth so easily beset us." Throw aside bitterness. Throw aside apathy. Throw aside complacency. Throw aside low self-esteem. Whatever is in between you and Jesus, throw it aside!

Bartimaeus threw his cloak aside and found himself standing before Jesus. As he stood there, Jesus asked him one question: "What do you want me to do for you?" Bartimaeus didn't have to scratch his head. He didn't have to think about it. He didn't have to ask his momma or his baby momma. He said, "Rabbi, let me recover my sight."

Be clear about what you want out of life. Know where you going. Set some goals. Choose a direction. Bartimaeus knew what he wanted and Jesus granted it. Jesus said to him, "Go your way, your faith has made you well." And the Bible says, "Immediately he recovered his sight!"

But notice that Bartimaeus didn't take Jesus up on his offer to "go his own way." Rather, once Bartimaeus recovered his sight, he didn't go do his own thing, he followed Jesus on the way! And when the Lord has made you an overcomer you ought not take his blessing and then go do your own thing. No, when the Lord has blessed your life you ought to commit your very life to Him!

Christ enables those who trust Him to overcome the defeating realities of our lives by healing our sight and granting us a new vision for life. Since I met Jesus, my life has changed. Because of Him I will never be the same.

Note

1. Horatius Bonar, "I Heard the Voice of Jesus Say."

# I Am Digging for Jesus

*Aaron McLeod*

Mark 2:1-12

**Brothers**, the word *dig* means to turn up, loosen, or remove earth. It means to advance by removing or pushing aside material. It also means to drive down so as to penetrate through some place, person, or thing. It also means to pay attention or to notice some place, person, or thing. As you know, the word dig is a verb. More pointedly, it is a transitive verb. And a transitive verb has two characteristics. First, it is an action verb which expressing a doable activity. Secondly, the transitive verb must have a direct object, which is something or someone who receives the action of the verb. To that end, I just don't say that *I dig*. I would say that *I dig dirt*, *I dig for gold, I dig her* or *I dig him*. For this homiletical excursion, I want to unpack how one might endeavor to dig for Jesus.

As we unpack this text, I want to point out four important themes. First, I want you to deal with the fact that paralysis is real in our community. Secondly, I will submit to you that there is power when you have the assistance of four men to effectuate community renewal. Thirdly, we must dismantle the crowds that keep people from Jesus. And finally, if you dig for Jesus, God will let you into the fullness of God's glory.

Brothers, our Scripture lesson comes from the Gospel of Mark, the shortest of the synoptic Gospels. This Gospel is distinguished from the other accounts because it is the oldest of the four Gospels, and it was probably the primary source of information for the writers of the Lukan and Matthian helms of the synoptic Gospels. Moreover, since neither Jesus nor his original disciples left any writings behind, the Gospel of Mark is the closest document to an original source on Jesus' life that currently exists since Mark was close to Peter, Jesus' closest disciple. Therefore many biblical scholars suggest that Mark is the New Testament historian who comes the closest to witnessing the actual life of Jesus.

At this juncture in the text in Mark 2, Jesus has developed a reputation for himself as a great healer. Jesus healed Peter's mother-in-law from migraines. Jesus has healed a man from leprosy. And people were extremely fascinated with this man from a ghetto called Nazareth. Jesus is preaching in a town called Capernaum, and people came to see his marvelous works. To this end, there was a paralytic who wanted to be healed by Jesus, but he could not get close to Jesus because of the crowd of nosey and messy onlookers. So four men lifted the paralytic to the top of the temple and began to dig a hole in the roof to lower the man to Jesus. The men lowered the paralytic to Jesus. Jesus forgave the paralytic of his sins because of his faith and Jesus healed his body and told him to walk, pick up his mat, and go home.

The Bible says that Jesus was preaching in Capernaum, the city of ancient Palestine on the northwest shore of Sea of Galilee. In our living context, Jesus was holding revival in an urban city like Los Angeles, Atlanta, Detroit, or Chicago. A paralyzed man heard Jesus was preaching in town and he wanted to be healed. The paralytic is nameless, but even though he is nameless, if Reverend Jesse Louis Jackson, Sr. were writing this sermon he would proclaim that this nameless paralytic is somebody. In light of his inherent anonymity, I am going to use my creative license and declare that the paralytic's first name is Johnny and his last name is Walker.

A paralytic is someone who has complete or partial loss of function especially when involving the motion or sensation in a part of the body. Normally paralytics are powerless or ineffective. In the text, the Greek translation is *paralytikos*. It means to suffer from the relaxing of the nerves whereby one's limbs are weak and unstable.

As I meditate on the text, I am convinced that Johnny Walker could actually walk. I suggest to you that Johnny Walker had no physical impairment, but he was spiritually immobile. He suffered from spiritual paralysis because his lifestyle did not allow him to walk in the fullness of God's Glory. Therefore, Johnny Walker was paralyzed.

Johnny Walker had a best friend named Jack Daniels. Johnny and Jack had a reputation for executing fraudulent activity around town. Johnny Walker was paralyzed.

Johnny Walker was married to a woman named Mary Jane. Everybody loved Mary Jane because she was always regarded as the life of the party. Even though Johnny was married to Mary Jane, he was not a family man because he had three mistresses: a French woman named Merlot, an American woman named Brandy, and a Mexican woman named

Margarita who Johnny liked a lot because he said she was very nice to him if he treated her to some salt on the rocks. Brothers, Johnny Walker was paralyzed.

Finally, Johnny Walker was irresponsible. He never kept a job longer than three months. He never paid his bills on time. He always borrowed money and never paid it back. Johnny Walker was paralyzed.

Brothers, like Johnny Walker, many of us in this challenging society are paralyzed. You may not suffer from being a liar, a cheat, a drunkard, a gigolo, or a womanizer like Johnny Walker, but you, too, are paralyzed. Let me break this down for you. In the words of Rev. Dr. Robin Smith, the beautiful African American sister who served as a resident psychologist on the *Oprah Winfrey Show,* some of us are paralyzed because we suffer from Miss Celie-itis (Whoopie Goldberg played Miss Celie and she was married to and abused by Mister, played by Danny Glover). Like Shug Avery in *The Color Purple*, somebody told you that you were ugly and you believed it. You are paralyzed. Like Mister in *The Color Purple*, someone told you that you would not amount to anything, that you are not special, that you have no worth, and you believed it. You are paralyzed.

Let me teach this like I mean it. Somebody said that you were too young to walk in the fullness of God's glory and to lead a ministry. They said nobody will follow you. Somebody said that you are too old and too technologically deficient to have an opinion in this age of iPads and iPhones. Somebody said that you are Black, and you can't break through the glass ceiling. And you believed them. Somebody said that you're not married and deduced that you are unstable to be trusted as a leader as a single person. Somebody said that you too educated or that you are not educated enough. Somebody said that you are wild or unruly because you are divorced and have had a failed marriage. Somebody said that you are wild as a single grown man. And you believed them.

Somebody said that you are cursed because you can't father children. Somebody said that you are tainted because you have too many children by several different women. And you believed them. You are paralyzed in your mind to let somebody else define who you are and your value as a person.

Brother, you may not be trifling like Johnny Walker or have low self-esteem like Miss Celie, but you are paralyzed because you lack faith. God said that you are the head and not the tail, but you seem more like the tail and not the head. You are robbing Peter to pay Paul. You are avoiding bill collectors like the plague. You are hiding your car from the repo man. You are using the generator to keep lights on in your place.

Instead of turning to Jesus, we are turning to fortune tellers to see when we are going to get out of our mess. We are paralyzed because we lack the faith. We don't believe that the earth is the Lord's and the fullness thereof. We are paralyzed because we lack the faith. We don't believe that Jesus will supply all our needs according to his riches and his glory. We are paralyzed because we lack the faith to recognize that if God be for us then God is more than the entire world against us. We are paralyzed because we lack the faith to recognize that God will never leave us or forsake us. We are paralyzed because we don't believe that all things work together for the good of them who love the Lord and who have been called to his purpose.

My beloved brothers, we are paralyzed because we lack the faith to work two jobs and go back to school so we can have better career prospects. Brothers, we are paralyzed because we lack the faith to start our own businesses despite the fact that we have been laid off or under-employed for several years. Black men, we are paralyzed because we lack the faith to cut off unhealthy intimate and platonic relationships (you know, those friends with benefits) that cause you stress rather than bring fulfillment. Brothers, we are paralyzed because we lack the faith to stand up and to lead the fight against the mis-education of our children, to combat drugs in our community, to dismantle the prison industrial complex, and to call out the racist, sexist, capitalist, classist, and uncompassionate folk (like Rush Limbaugh, Glenn Beck, Mark Levin, and Bill O'Reilly) who still question the leadership of our re-elected President Barack Hussein Obama, the one who bailed out the banks, the one who saved the auto industry, the one who gave us healthcare reform, the one captured Osama Bin Ladin, the one who created green jobs, and the one who is working to reform the student loan crisis that has crippled so many deserving students who could not afford to subsidize their college education.

Brother, you may not be trifling like Johnny Walker; you may not have low self-esteem like Miss Celie; and you may not lack faith, but you are paralyzed because you are disheartened because you have not realized the dreams for your life. Your friends are happy and you are miserable. People are getting promotions and you got your pink slip. Your boy married a Proverbs 31 woman, but you are on the sidelines running from Boo Boo. Although, you are a hard-working brother you haven't been able to solidify a meaningful relationship with a goodhearted and unselfish sister who loves the Lord more than anything in the world. Now, you have studied hard and earned three or four degrees from great schools, however things have not taken off for you although they've taken off for everyone else. And I can go on and on. It's not working for you, and you are fed up.

Just maybe, you are paralyzed because you don't fast, you don't meditate, and you are impatient. You are paralyzed because you will not turn down your plate for one or two meals per day. You will not turn off Facebook, Twitter, or Instagram. You will not turn off your devices and fall on your knees and pray, *"Father, I stretch my hands to Thee; No other help I know. If Thou withdraw Thyself from me, O! whither shall I go?"*[1] You will not sing, *"Precious Lord, take my hand, Lead me on, help me stand; I am tired, I am weak, I am worn; Through the storm, through the night, Lead me on to the light, Take my hand, precious Lord, lead me home."*[2]

Brother, you must be confident in the fact that your paralysis is only a test that you're going through. And, it will be over real soon. Trials come just to make you strong. Be strong, keep the faith, don't give up, and realize it's only a test you're going through.[3]

I submit to you that your paralysis can be temporary. It's simply up to you to decide if you will allow it to be your reality or not. Transitioning back to the text, our friend Johnny Walker realized that his life was in shambles, and he wanted to turn his situation around. Johnny heard about this man named Jesus. The text says that Johnny Walker found four men and he pleaded with them to take him to Jesus. Brothers, I want to park right here parenthetically to ask the question, why did Johnny Walker call on four men? Arguably, Johnny Walker could have called on these men because, as men, they were supposed to be priests, providers, and protectors of the village. Well, even though he chose men, my question now is, Why did he choose *four* men? The number four is significant for many reasons. Biblically, four denotes God's *creative works*. On the *fourth* day God created the sun, moon, and stars and set them in the vault of heaven to give light on earth to have charge over day and night and to separate light from darkness. Additionally, *four* is the number of the great elements: Earth, Air, Fire, and Water. There are four regions of the earth: North, South, East, and West. There are four divisions of the day: Morning, Noon, Evening, and Midnight. There are four seasons of the year: Winter, Spring, Summer, and Fall.

I don't know about you but, like the paralytic in the text whom we are calling Johnny Walker, I could use four men to get some meaningful tasks done in the community. I could use four good men to pray and teach and agree with me about the state of our community, in particular public education. I could use four good men to give two hours per week to ensure that our children can read. I could use four good Black men to marry and love unconditionally four good Black women to ensure that we are preserving the finer qualities of the Black family. I could use four good men to police our neighborhoods in effort to stop violence and help our young people resolve their differences without using their fists and guns. I could use four good men who will hold four other brothers accountable to treat ours sisters as equals and support them and empower them versus demonizing them and exploiting them. I could use four good men who will who will lead a fatherhood campaign across this country to motivate men to take care of their children, to love their children, to protect their children, and to be like Jesus' daddy, Joseph, and even be willings to raise another man's baby because it's the right thing to do.

I could use four good men to challenge the ignorance, uncompassionate nature, and buffoonery of Rush Limbaugh, Mark Levin, Glenn Beck, Sean Hannity, Bill O'Reilly, and most sadly the religious leader, Franklin Graham. I could use four good men who will march across this country and remind America of the grave injustice of how an innocent Black boy named Trayvon Martin armed with candy and a jar of iced tea is murdered while a crazy and deranged man named George Zimmerman goes free under the auspices of the stand-your-ground law that is obtuse and sloppy to say the least. I could use four men to lead a national movement proclaiming that Black lives matter in light of the miscalculated deaths of Michael Brown, Eric Gardner, and Tamir Rice. Can God get four good men? Four men represent hope.

In the text, the paralytic took action to seek help to change his situation. Men, it is imperative that we make ourselves available to give hope a chance in an effort to change our collective situation? Will you give hope a chance and enroll in school to change the reality of your life? Will you give hope a chance and take on a second job to pay off your credit cards to save money to purchase your own property? Will you give hope a chance and lead your family and friends to church? Will you give hope a chance and forgive those who spitefully used you and show them the love of Christ?

The Bible says that Johnny Walker could not get to Jesus because of the crowd. Here the Greek translation for the word crowd is *ochlos*, which means a casual collection of common people who are ignorant. In my particular opinion, I feel that the crowd was a distraction and a hindrance for Johnny Walker to get closer to Jesus and hear him preach the word of God. The crowd was not there to be redeemed, but they were there to be nosey and to get in the way of Johnny Walker's soul salvation.

In the crowd, Johnny saw some of the people who encouraged his insignificant behavior. In the crowd, Johnny saw old drinking buddies, girlfriends, and hustling partners. Brothers, don't get it twisted – there were some church people in the crowd as well. These people are the keepers of religious regularity. Sneaky Steward and Trustworthy Trustee were in crowd. This was the steward who is dedicated to demonizing and degrading others and this was trustee who always developed traps to highlight the transgressions of others. The Pseudo Preacher was in the crowd as well. This is the preacher who lies on Monday, cheats on Tuesday, steals on Wednesday, gambles on Thursday, parties on Friday, shacks on Saturday, and preaches on Sunday.

If church folk are not careful, we, too, can be a part of the crowd who prevents paralyzed people from getting close to Jesus and hearing a word from the Lord. So the question for us today is will we leave the crowd and be like the four men who helped the paralytic and bring paralyzed people to Jesus to be healed? Johnny Walker found four men and he pleaded with them to lift him above the crowd, because Johnny knew if he was going to get to Jesus he would have to rise above the crowd. So when Johnny Walker rose above the crowd, the Bible says a path was dug through the roof for him to connect with Jesus and be healed. Like Johnny Walker, we too have to dig paths through unnecessary barriers in our church that keep people from God, from the word of God, and from walking in the fullness of God's glory.

Brothers, we must be careful, even within the church. Some church folks can be some of the meanest and nastiest folks that you ever want to deal with. You-name-its are here: racism, sexism, ageism, beautyism, xenophobism, homophobism, heterosexism. As men, we can not sit back and let these injustices prevail on our watch. Jesus would not have let that go on.

Well, I met Johnny Walker a few days ago and I asked him a profound question about his digging experience: "Johnny, how did you dig for Jesus?" Johnny said, "Brother preacher, first I had to relinquish my membership at Bedside Baptist Church. Then I had to stop making regular visits to Pillow Pentecostal Church, Comfortable Couch Community Church, and Full Futon Faithful Fellowship on Sunday mornings. I had to make a commitment to push my way to church on Sunday mornings and Wednesday nights for prayer service and Bible study, and to serve God with my whole heart. When I did this I felt myself digging closer to Jesus. Then I grew closer to God and my worship became real. I began to thank God because nobody called my mother and said her baby had a bullet in his head. I began to thank God because despite my shiftlessness and selfishness, God kept food on my table."

Then I said, "Brother Johnny Walker, what did you do next?" Johnny said, "I kept on digging for Jesus. I cut inconsequential people and bad habits out of my diet. I don't hang around Jack Daniels, Smirnoff, Courvoisier, or my Dutch cousin, Heineken, anymore. I recognized that LL Cool J was wrong when he said I needed an '*Around the Way Girl*' because they caused most of my problems. So I cut off all the those girls from around the way. Instead of going to the club, I went to prayer meeting; instead of going to gamble, I went to Bible study; and instead of staying out all night, I came home at night and went to bed and went to work on time in the morning. I changed my ways and I felt myself digging closer to Jesus. I prayed for the Holy Ghost to come upon me so I could receive power from God and that made all the difference. I had power to live right, to treat my neighbor right, to do right, to love my enemies, to deny myself for the benefit of others, to speak things that were not as if they were so, and to fight through my tears and disappointments and persevere toward the mark of the high calling."

Then I asked Johnny Walker what happened when he finally made contact with Jesus. Johnny said, "Jesus picked me up, he turned me around, and he placed my feet on a solid ground. Jesus gave me a new name. People no longer call me Johnny Walker. Now my first name is *Been* and my last name is *Redeemed*. Jesus gave me a new walk and I don't go places I used to go. Jesus gave me a peace in my life that passes all understanding."

Finally, I asked Brother Been Redeemed to give me a word of encouragement for the men who may read this book and may be facing trials and tribulations. Brother Been Redeemed told me to tell you to rejoice in the fact that we serve a God who is able to do exceedingly and abundantly above all that we ask or think, *according to the power that worketh in us*. (Ephesians 3:20)

In the words of Dr. Gina Stewart, God is able to give us power to face the storms and the staggering disappointments of our life. God is able to give us the inner equilibrium to stand tall amid the trials and burdens of life. God is able to provide inner peace amid our storms. So keep digging for Jesus.

When I look back over my life, and I begin to think things over, I can truly say that I have been blessed because I serve a God who is able. Brothers, we serve a God who able to pick you up, turn you around, and place your feet on a solid ground. We serve a God who is able to give sunshine on a cloudy day. We serve a God who is able to give unspeakable joy. Our God is able. So keep digging for Jesus.

I can testify that Jesus is bread when I am hungry. Jesus is water when I am thirsty. He is worthy of all the praise. Keep digging for Jesus.

He is a waymaker and caretaker. He has been a mind regulator and a heavy load sharer. He is worthy of all the praise. Keep digging for Jesus. He is my strength for today and my hope for tomorrow because we call him Wonderful Counselor, Mighty God, Everlasting Father, and Prince of Peace. Keep digging for Jesus.

> *Living He loved me,*
> *dying He saved me,*
> *buried He carried my sins far away.*
> *Rising He justified, freed me for heaven.*
> *One day He's coming back, glorious day.*[4]

And that's why I dig for Jesus and praise His Holy Name, because all things are possible through Christ Jesus.

## Notes

1.  Charles Wesley, "Father, I Stretch My Hands to Thee."
2.  Thomas A. Dorsey, "Precious Lord, Take My Hand."
3.  Larry Trotter, "It's Only a Test."
4.  J. Wilbur Chapman, "One Day."

# When Men Stand Up

*Lester A. McCorn*

Luke 19:1-10

*Jesus* was on a mission. He possessed a sense of urgency, which was two-fold: he was going to Jerusalem to be offered as a ransom for many, and he was confronting the kingdom of this world (political, spiritual, and economic). But in between Calvary and the Kingdom, I believe that Jesus had a third, major motive in mind: to make men stand up. You may think this is exegetical heresy or hermeneutical hyperbole, but I just believe that Jesus had a mission to make men stand up!

Jesus was on a mission. Reaching Jericho, Jesus continued his journey up the dangerous hills toward Jerusalem. Jericho was a city located on the west side of the Jordan River about five miles (8 kilometers) from the southernmost fords (or shallow places) and about ten miles (16 kilometers) northwest of the Dead Sea. Being in the broad part of the plain of the Jordan, Jericho lies nearly 1,000 feet (305 meters) below sea level and about 3,500 feet (1,067 meters) below Jerusalem, which was a mere 17 miles (27 kilometers) away. Jericho is the place that Jesus references in his parable about a man on the dangerous slope of the Jericho Road who is robbed, beaten, and left for dead. Holy men, including a priest and a rabbi pass him by on this road. But a Good Samaritan stops by to help. This time there is a man at the end of the road who is wounded, but doesn't know how badly wounded he is. There is a man at the end of the road who needs help but doesn't know how badly he needs it. And, there is a holy man coming up the road who will not only help him and heal him, but ultimately will deliver him.

Jesus had made it up the road and was on his way. By the time he got to Jericho, a crowd had found him and pressed him. Interruption came before Jesus could leave the city. A clever tax collector was determined to see Jesus. As an administrator for the Roman government's tax office, Zacchaeus had amassed great wealth by overcharging the Jewish people and taking a cut from the taxes gathered by other tax collectors whose work he administered. His wealth, however, could not provide the one thing he wanted and needed more than anything else. Unable to see over or get through the massive crowd swarming around Jesus, Zacchaeus noted the direction Jesus was taking, ran ahead, found a tree, and climbed up into its branches.[1]

Now I have to give Zacchaeus credit for taking initiative: He obviously knew that there was something lacking in his life. Like many men, we know there's a problem but we hope that no one else can see it. But it's so obvious that others' perception of us prevents us from fulfilling our potential. Instead of our future, others can see only our failures. Instead of our promise, they can see only our problems. Instead of our success, they can see only our setbacks. We think we've covered up our mess with mammon and material only to discover that our soul is naked as a jaybird, and our spirit is dry as dust. There are some things that Sean John can't conceal. There are some things that Tom Ford can't hide, and Aeropostle and Abercrombie can't cover. There are some things that Coach and Gucci can't disguise.

The Bible says that Zacchaeus could not see Jesus. We have concluded that he couldn't see him because he was short in stature. But his height was not the only reason he couldn't see Jesus. *He couldn't see him because he couldn't stand up.* He was a professional success but a private failure. He was financially wealthy but morally bankrupt. He was politically astute but spiritually deficient. Being a tax collector was one of the most vilified and despised positions in the Jewish community. Tax collectors were Public Enemy #1. They were pawns of the government, parasites of the economic system, and pariahs of the indigenous community. Zacchaeus could have helped to change the system, but instead he perpetuated it and profited from it. He couldn't see Jesus because he was a small man.

Somehow, Zacchaeus had the wherewithal to get ahead of the crowd. That was always his strategy. He perceived where Jesus was going and positioned himself where he could see Jesus. What he had not figured on was that Jesus would see him. Zacchaeus climbed up, as he had always done, to get a competitive advantage in life, only to have Jesus call him down to change his life.

"Zacchaeus, come down now! I'm coming to your house." And Zacchaeus got down with a quickness and gladly received Jesus into his home. And the Bible said, "They all murmured and complained." *They* said, "How's he gonna go to his house? Doesn't he know that he's a sinner? Jesus ought to know better than that." My first question is, *Who is they?* You always gonna have to deal with *they*. They are going to know your business. They are going to know your past. They are going to know your reputation. They are going to know what you are not and what you deserve and who you deserve to be with. They were just hating 'cause Jesus didn't ask to go to their house.

Jesus was about to make Zacchaeus stand up. And Jesus has the power to turn a small man into a big man who is unafraid to stand up.

### A Direct Confrontation

The first thing that happened was a direct confrontation. Jesus called Zacchaeus by name. Jesus wasn't scared. This wasn't just man to man, but man to system. It was people versus Powers; kingdom vs. Kingdom. This was a direct confrontation, not an altercation. Today, men, instead of blind allegiance or uncritical conformity, we need a direct confrontation.

We are facing the worst wealth disparity we've faced in generations, and the Republicans have the nerve to say that President Obama has incited and instigated class warfare. They started class warfare when they adopted policies that favored big corporations and wealthy millionaires and billionaires with tax loopholes and exemptions. They started it when they created a permanent underclass of people trapped in poverty because of a system that shreds the safety net and then labels you unfit to swim. And now the middle class is sinking. And they wonder why there has been an "Occupy Wall Street" movement. We need to Occupy Wall Street and Main Street and Bank of America Street and Wells Fargo Street. We need to occupy until socio-economic justice rolls down like waters and fiscal righteousness like a mighty stream!

The only way to change the system is to confront it. You cannot change what you will not confront. Stop complaining about "the man" and stop screaming about "the conspiracy." Call a spade a spade, let go of your diamonds, Jack, and get a heart, and summon your Kings and Queens to get that Joker and declare war!

Jesus called Zacchaeus by name because he wanted to remind him of who he was. He was a Jew just like the folk he was exploiting. But he was not going to be allowed to go on like that anymore.

We don't need to only confront the "enemy." We need to confront some of our own. Our men need to be confronted about their complacency and complicity. Our communities are also suffering because we don't have enough men standing up. We have left our neighborhoods unprotected, our women uncovered, our schools under-resourced, our churches unsupported, and our children unguarded. Our children are vulnerable, victimized, and voiceless. The predators of the world can get to our children because our men are missing in action. Human trafficking is proliferating at alarming numbers. Predators know they can exploit and molest our children because they are economically vulnerable and socially exposed. We need to have a respectable direct confrontation with our brothers.

### A Deliberate Conversation

We don't need a monologue, but a deliberate dialogue. Let's eavesdrop on the conversation between Jesus and Zacchaeus. It was just man to man, no representatives, no handlers, no agents, no entourage. Let's talk about what's going on in our community. What has happened in Ferguson and New York and Cleveland and Baltimore has awakened a sleeping giant. And the uprisings are more than riots, they are a call to conversation. Dr. Martin Luther King said, "Riots are the language of the unheard." We need to listen before we talk. But there is an adage that says, "People don't care how much you know until they know how much you care." Before we talk to our brothers we need to show them that we love them. We need to show up for them. We need to speak up for them. We need to stand up for them! We need to have some deliberate conversations with the powers and people that threaten our existence. Just like Jesus had a conversation with Zacchaeus, we need to have a conversation with our brothers.

We need to have a deliberate conversation with George Zimmerman about Trayvon Martin.

We need to have a deliberate conversation with Michael Dunn about Jordan Davis.

We need to have a deliberate conversation with the cops who killed Eric Garner.

We need to have a deliberate conversation with the cops who killed Tamir Rice.

We need to have a deliberate conversation with the cops who killed Freddie Gray.

We need to have some deliberate conversations with our adversaries, antagonists, attackers, and accusers, like Jesus had with Zacchaeus. After we've had a direct confrontation and a deliberate conversation, we need to move towards a divine conciliation.

### A Divine Conciliation

This was a reunion between saint and sinner. Zacchaeus was used to being the boss. He was used to bringing the heat, putting on the pressure. He was the Man.

But Jesus' confrontation and conversation led Zacchaeus to conciliation. He wanted to make up for what he had done. He was being reunited with his people and reconciled to God.

Something happened between verse 7 and verse 8. I wish I could have heard their conversation. I'm not sure what was said, but I saw something in verse 8 that I never realized before. It says, "Zacchaeus stood up." Little Zack became Big Zacchaeus.

In order to say yes, Zacchaeus had to say no to some other things. Not a plea bargain, but a divine conciliation. This was a moment of decision. And Zacchaeus decided to be a man. He was risking his position. He was risking his portfolio. He was risking his prominence. But this moment led him to do the right thing. He stood up.

Today, my brothers, we have to decide if we're going to be a man and stand up. But I must warn you that it is dangerous when you stand up. They will try to kill you when you stand up.

They killed Medgar Evers for standing up. They killed Malcolm X for standing up. They killed Martin Luther King for standing up. They killed Stephen Biko for standing up. But stand anyhow. Dr. King said, "Every man should have something to die for. A man who won't die for something isn't fit to live."

God has a way of getting us to stand up in spite of the opposition we are facing, because there is something within us that just won't let us stay down for long.

I know you remember the story of little Johnny who was rambunctious and disobedient in class. His teacher told him several times, "Johnny sit down. Johnny sit down!" But when Johnny refused to sit down, his teacher walked over to him and physically pushed him down into his seat. And Johnny looked at her defiantly and said, "I may be sitting down on the outside but I'm standing up on the inside!"

Today, in spite of all we've been through, I'm glad to report that we're still standing up. Persecution, opposition, discrimination, lynching, execution, assassination, intimidation, terrorization, oppression, and depression . . . but we're still standing up!

But I need to tell you what happened to Johnny later on. Because Johnny was so rambunctious and defiant he refused to move after the teacher made him sit down, when it was time to participate in a class assignment the teacher asked Johnny to stand up with some of his other classmates. But Johnny said, "No, you made me sit down, so I'm gonna sit down." The teacher said, "Johnny, I'm not playing with you. I said, stand up!" But Johnny refused to do what the teacher said. So the teacher said, "Don't make me do what you don't want me to do." Johnny said, "What you gonna do?" And the teacher pulled out her phone and said, "Fine, I'll just call your daddy." And before the teacher got to the third digit, Johnny jumped up out his chair and hollered, "No, no. Please whatever you do, don't call my daddy! I'll do what you say do, I'll stand up. Just don't call my daddy."

Men, it's time to stand up! Why are you still sitting down?! Don't make me call your heavenly daddy! It's time to stand up.

But it's not only time for you to stand up. It's time for you to get your brothers to stand up! And I've got a strategy for you to get your brothers to stand up. I'm going to give you the key. You don't need a gimmick. You don't need a bribe. You don't need trickery. You don't need the Players Club. You don't need someone to shake their money maker. What you need is a key. You want the key? Here it is:

> *How to reach the masses, men of every birth,*
> *For an answer Jesus gave the key:*
> *"And I, if I be lifted up from the earth,*
> *Will draw all men unto Me."*

*Lift Him up! Lift Him up!*
*Lift the precious Savior up,*
*Lift the precious Savior up,*
*Still He speaks from eternity:*
*"And I, if I be lifted up from the earth,*
*Will draw all men unto Me."*

*Oh! the world is hungry for the Living Bread,*
*Lift the Savior up for them to see;*
*Trust Him, and do not doubt the words that He said,*
*"I'll draw all men unto Me."*[2]

You want your friend to stand up? Lift him up.
You want your relative to stand up? Lift him up.
You want your son to stand up? Lift him up.
You want your brother to stand up? Lift him up.
Don't cuss him out. Lift him up.
Don't beat him down. Lift him up.
Don't trip him up. Lift him up.

I know you're saying, "But the odds are against us. We've been demonized and dehumanized. We've been victimized and vilified. We've been castrated and emasculated. We've been anesthetized and desensitized. It's almost impossible to get our men to stand up."

But there was another man who was placed upon another tree. He did not climb up there like Zacchaeus. But they hung him on a tree. However, they made one major mistake. They should have left him on the ground to die. But they made the mistake of lifting him up.

And when you lift him up, you make demons flee.
When you lift him up, you make kingdoms crumble.
When you lift him up, you make your enemies behave.
When you lift him up, you make your haters back up.
When you lift him up, you make your troubles cease
When you lift him up, you make your storm clouds pass away.

Notes

1. T. C. Butler, Vol. 3: Luke (Nashville, TN: Broadman & Holman Publishers, 2000), 314.
2. Johnson Oatman Jr., "Lift Him Up."

# The Man Who Finds Favor with God

*James Perkins*

Genesis 6:9

***Should*** the providence of God allow the world to stand for another ten thousand times ten thousand years, we will never be able to repay the incalculable debt we owe to those people who have protested, resisted, critiqued, and refused to be comfortable with the prevailing spirit of their day and generation. Life is worth living and the world is a decent place to live because there have always been people who refused to fit in and merely go along with the trend of the times. There have always been people who were governed by a higher set of principles, whose souls have been hypnotized by a heavenly vision, and whose allegiance has been to a higher reality than what they saw and experienced around them.

There is so much pressure to conform to the fads and fashions of the times and to be numbered among the "in crowd" that it takes a strong person to stand up, to stand alone, and to stand firmly on the solid ground of their own convictions. Most people are afraid to stand up and speak out on a given issue because they fear being ostracized and criticized. They can't handle the verbal backlash that inevitably comes when you seek to be your own person. When you don't look like everybody else, when you don't sound like a remix of everybody else, when you're not a carbon copy of everybody else, people will call you an oddball and a screwball. They will say unkind things to and about you. They will ridicule and poke fun at you to such an extent that you won't want to dare to be different even when being different is just being who you are.

We live in a world where everybody is always trying to squeeze us into their little mold and to make us in the image and after the likeness of the popular image of the time. In this time, boys are supposed to look and act like thugs and girls are supposed to look and act like questionable women. And if they can fit that image, imitate that behavior, and project that model, they can be popular, they can be accepted, and they can be a part of the crowd. It's no fun to be unpopular; to be made to feel like you're a freak and a misfit. And so everybody just fits in and goes along.

But there comes a time in each of our lives when we must decide whether we're going to live by the opinions of others, or whether we're going to live on the basis of our own convictions. And when you choose to live on the basis of your own convictions, when you can look at the situation and decide you're going to do something else, you can expect to be criticized by the crowd, to be ridiculed and talked about.

It's tough, but, there is no better feeling and there is no greater evidence of favor on your life than having the strength to hang on to your own convictions even in the midst of a hatin' mess.

One of the most stressful challenges we all face is the challenge of dealing with the power of peer pressure. All of us want to be accepted. All of us want the approval of others. But sometimes in order to gain the acceptance and approval of others, it means that we have to sell a little piece of our soul and sacrifice what we believe in and whom God wants us to be.

Have you ever done that? Have you ever done something stupid just so you could feel like you belonged? Peer pressure says there are certain things you must do if you want to be a part of the group. Peer pressure says there are certain values that you can't have if you're going to be a part of the gang. Peer pressure says there is a certain way that you must look, dress, and talk if you're going to be down with it! And these things are not always positive and beneficial.

A whole lot of people have ruined their lives and never experienced the favor of God on their life because they couldn't resist the powerful influence of peer pressure. Some people developed a drug habit because peer pressure said it was cool to do drugs. Some baby mamas and baby daddys have brought a whole lot of unwanted, unparented, and unloved babies into this cold and cruel world because peer pressure said it's cool to do it! A whole lot of young bruhs have ended up in prison because peer pressure said it's cool to pack a gun, to rob, or to kill.

Peer pressure is a strong influence, but it's not always a positive. All of us are influenced by somebody. We do not develop our values and shape our opinions apart from the input of other people. But we must not allow the influence of others to be so strong in our lives that to please our peers, to find acceptance, and to experience a sense of belonging, we become willing to sell our souls and destroy who we are.

Who we are is not who people say we are. Who we are is not who people want us to be. Who we are is not even who we think we are. Who we are is who God created us to be and who God says we are! And we must never run the risk of losing God's favor and give up who we are and what we believe in order to satisfy other people.

It doesn't matter what goes down; ultimately you will be held responsible for your own actions. We need to be reminded of this little sobering fact of life because we love to blame everybody else for what we did and what's wrong with us. Your friends may agitate and encourage you to do wrong, but you'll have to face the consequences all by yourself. Your friends may get you into trouble, but they won't be there to help get you out of trouble. Your friends can't live for you. Your friends can't die for you. Your friends can't right your wrong for you. You can give in to the negative influence of others if you choose, but you'll have to face the music, pay the piper, shoulder the shame, and face the consequences all by yourself!

The tendency to just give in and go along with negative influence has allowed an unhealthy environment to grow up all around us! Blind uncritical participation in the popular culture of the time has allowed a steady stream of unhealthy attitudes and behaviors make decency and righteousness look like an oddball and unfavored behavior. When you're trying to do the right thing and it seems like you're getting nowhere; when everybody else is doing their own thing and succeeding, it looks like they have favor and you don't!

At some point, there needs to be a groundswell of protest. There needs to be an uprising on the part of the people of God. We need to protest unrighteousness, picket corruption, and chase spiritual wickedness from high and low places.

Evil environments grow up around us because nobody has the courage to stand up and say no! Self-destructive behavior sabotages our lives because we indulge our urges and impulses instead of finding the strength to say no! Greed has taken over because too many people are too selfish to say no!

The greater tragedy is that the religion of our time has become weak, impotent, and ineffective. We have lost the protest spirit. We no longer speak out against injustice and social evils. The Church has capitulated to culture. We have caved in to status quo. We are more concerned about empty praise than we are about righteous protest. We are more concerned about our individual prosperity than we are about community economic development. We are more concerned about being in style than we are about being in the Spirit. We are more concerned about being popular than we are about being right.

There's something wrong when men don't have enough courage to stand up for what is right and to stand up for God. God's men don't cave in. God's men are not afraid of the status quo. God's men are supposed to set the agenda and not go along with the world's agenda.

But now many of our men are quiet and passive. We act like we have struck a deal with the devil. We act like we're afraid that if we don't go with the flow, if we're out of step with the style, people will call us an oddball, a square, or a misfit.

But history seems to demonstrate that God has a certain attraction for little righteous oddballs and little moral misfits. We may not understand it, but God seems to show favor to the Moses, the Martin, the Malcolm, and the Mandela types.

It isn't that God isn't attracted to everybody. It's just that He can't create a spiritual revolution with people who are too scared to move. Status quo people haven't ever been any help when it comes to building the Kingdom of God! The people who find favor with God are people who didn't mind being called an oddball. And there have been these peculiar and obtuse types in every generation.

The society may call them rejects, religious maniacs, and all sorts of names, but God always seem to have found favor with them and made room for them on His agenda. It was because Abraham was so strange that he was willing to pull up stakes and follow the voice of God not knowing where he was to go that God found favor with him and said, "I can use a man like that to teach the world a lesson about faith." It was after Moses had killed an oppressive Egyptian that God found favor with him and said, "I need a man like this to teach the world a lesson about justice!" It was when Habakkuk climbed to the top of his tower although the fig tree did not blossom and there were no herds in the stalls that God found favor with him and said, "I can use a man like that to teach the world a lesson about hope."

It seems like the crazier they are, the more peculiar they are, the more determined they are to swim against the tide of the times, the more willing God seems to be willing to show them favor and put them to work on the Kingdom construction crew. If the world calls you an oddball, a screwball, or a misfit, chances are that God is saying, "That's the man I want."

Well, just a few generations after the creation of Adam, God decided that in making humanity, He had made a dreadful mistake. The saddest word in the whole Bible is that "The Lord was sorry that He had made man on the earth, and it grieved Him to His heart" (Genesis 6:6). Think of this! Humanity – crowned with glory and honor! Humanity – given power and dominion! Humanity – now spoiled with sin, crooked by perversion, ruined beyond redemption!

And the tragedy is that even in our time, we don't seem to be any better. When we see how evil our society has become, all the violence, and all the corruption, we can't help but wonder how it can get any worse.

It made God sorry that He had made humanity. God, who cannot make a mistake, regretted that He had created human life. It made God feel like maybe He had made a mistake after all.

And I don't know about you, but I don't want God to look at me and feel like He made a mistake. I know I'm all messed up and conflicted on the inside. Even when I would do good, evil is always with me. But I don't want Him to feel like He made a mistake. I know that I'm not as faithful as I should be, or as committed as I need to be, but I don't want Him to look at me and feel like He made a mistake. I know my tendency is to do wrong even though my desire is to do right, but I just don't want Him to look at me and feel like He made a mistake.

God looked at His world and decided that the only solution was to flush the first creation; to get some soap, a mop, and a bucket and clean up the mess humanity had made. God decided to destroy the world, but there was one man, one lone oddball sort of a fellow, whom God said He could use in His judgment and redemption program.

When everybody else was jamming, this man was praising. When they were busy trying to build a reputation, this man was busy trying to build an altar. When they were networking and courting corrupt associates, this man was walking and talking with God!

And so, God showed favor and said, "I can use this man to be sort of a second father of the human race. I can start over with him."

The earth was corrupt. The society was shot through with sin. The world was going to hell in a hand basket. "But Noah found favor in the eyes of the Lord." (Genesis 6:9)

Noah was an oddball in his day. And as God's people, if you want to find favor with God, we must be willing to be so radically obedient to God that in the eyes of the world we are perceived as strange spiritual oddballs. That's the way Noah was. He stood out from among all the people of his day and generation.

There are some characteristics that Noah had that we must seek to imitate if we, like him, want God's favor.

### He Lived an Alternative Lifestyle

One of the qualities that attracted God to Noah was the fact that he didn't live like everybody else. Everybody else was caught up and hung up on trying to be in tune with the times. But while everybody was trying to be hip, Noah was out there trying to be holy! The word of our text is that "Noah walked with God." He lived an alternative lifestyle. He lived a holy lifestyle. And, my brothers, at some point we've got to recognize that this Christian life is a call to live a holy life. Not holy in the sense that you're more perfect than everybody else, but holy in the sense that we're earnestly trying to live life God's way. If we're not at least putting forth our best efforts to live a holy life, we can't position ourselves to experience the yoke-breaking power of God in our lives.

Some of us have been wrestling with the same demons for years, and we don't have the power to expel them out of our life because we have our name on the church roll but no God in our hearts! We're not supposed to be more worldly than the people in the world. We're supposed to live in an order that can show others the way of holiness. The young brothers need to be shown a different way!

It's bad when there is no discernible difference between the lifestyle of the people of the world and the lifestyle of the people of God. It's bad when you can't tell who's who! Our lifestyle ought to set us apart because we've got God's favor!

Holiness is a way of walking! Holiness is a way of talking! Holiness is a way of living! As men of God, every day our prayer ought to be, "Lord, I want to be holy in my heart." Now, I know that isn't popular, but it sure is right!

That was the problem in the days of Noah. On the surface everything looked fine. The stock market was up. They had a bulging middle class. Everybody was doing fine. In fact, that was the problem. They were doing so well that you couldn't tell who was whom! The fine line of spiritual distinction had been erased. Everything had just become acceptable. There was no wrong anymore! You couldn't tell the righteous men from the wretched men! They all looked the same. They all acted the same!

Some said they were God's people. They even went to church. But there was no difference in the way they lived. They read the Bible as a religious recreational exercise, but they didn't live the Bible as a lifestyle. They said their prayers, but they didn't pray! They wanted to be socially up to date, but while they were busy being up to date, sin was spreading. Families were fizzling.

Old Noah was the preacher, but he had to have church by himself. The old preachers used to say that Noah preached 120 years and didn't get a convert! He didn't have but one sermon. Every time he opened his mouth all he would say is, "God said it's gonna rain!"

The folks called Noah crazy because it had never rained before, and the sky was still cloudless and blue. They laughed at Noah and joked about the size of the boat he was building. They had never seen a boat of such magnitude before. Nobody listened, but still Noah walked with God. And that's the lifestyle we must live. We've got to walk with God!

People may call you a religious fanatic, but walk with God. We can't shape our lives on the value system of the world; shape your values on the Word of God. We've got to save the world by showing them a holy lifestyle. We've got to walk with God!

Be a rebel for righteousness. Walk with God every day; all day! When you walk with Him, He'll lead you beside still waters. When you walk with Him, He'll prepare you a table in the presence of your enemies. When you walk with Him, He'll chase failure and misery out of your life and make joy bells ring down deep in your soul!

I don't know about you, but I'm going to walk with Him, talk with Him, pray to Him, live for Him, praise His name. I'm going to walk with God!

### He Had the Courage to Stand Alone

Another characteristic of men who find favor with God is that they have the courage to stand alone. The text says, "But Noah . . ."

No other names are mentioned. Just a lone, single, solitary individual. "But Noah . . ." Everybody else was busy trying to be up with the time, doing everything it was popular to do, but Noah said, "I'm going to walk with God if I have to walk with Him by myself! I'm going to live for Him if I have to live for Him by myself!"

And, my brothers, you find God's favor when you have the courage of your convictions. There ought to be something that you believe in so strongly that you'll stick to it even if it means that you are all by yourself.

The people tried to talk Noah into going along with them. They laughed at him. They dismissed him as being a nut. They said he was crazy. But Noah said, "You can call me any name you want to, but I'm going to walk with God if I have to walk with Him by myself!"

Noah had the courage of his convictions. And all oddballs have the courage to stand alone and go on and do whatever they have to do even if they have to do it by themselves. You can't stand around and wait for people to get ready to serve the Lord before you turn from your wicked ways and serve Him. You've got to go on and serve the Lord even if you have to serve Him by yourself. You can't wait on people to give you the go ahead to go on and get your life together. If you wait on people to make up their mind before you do anything, you'll never get anything done. If you're going to do anything with yourself, you've got to go ahead and do it even if it means you have to do it by yourself.

Men, most of us can't even really be the kind of Christians we ought to be because we don't have the courage to stand alone. We're always taking our cues from the crowd. We always hesitate to make a decision, talking about we want to be on the right side. And what that means for most of us is the side that most people are on. We can't stand to be by ourselves, right or wrong!

Even in the church, we can't stand to be alone. Before we do anything, we look around to see if anybody else is doing something before we will because we don't want to get caught standing by ourselves. But in evil times, in sinful time, in all times, you have to have the courage to stand for right and righteousness, even if you have to stand by yourself.

Noah was all by himself. The world was against him, but heaven was present. No man stood with him, but God was on his side and he found favor with God. And if God be for you, who can be against you!

As men, we've got to practice the courage of our convictions so we can teach it to our children. They have a lot more to contend with at their age than we did! We've got to teach them to resist the temptation to get involved with drugs and all the stuff people try to pressure them to do. They need to be encouraged to stand if they have to stand alone.

Stand for right. Stand for scholarship. Stand for cleanness. Stand for goodness. Don't be afraid to take a stand even if it means you've got to stand all by yourself. Sly and the Family Stones used to sing a song, "Stand, and in the end you'll still be you. One whose done all the things you set out to do. Stand."

Brothers, don't get tangled up with the evils of this age all in the name of being cool and being in style. Don't settle to just have your name on the church roll but not really commit to living the life. Stand for integrity. Stand for virtue. Stand for morality. Stand for decency. Stand for Jesus even if it means that you have to stand all by yourself!

Don't seek to be popular. Seek to be prophetic. Politicians strive to be popular. These politicians will change everything they believe in if it will get them two points in the public opinion polls. Noah wasn't trying to be popular. He said in essence, "I don't care about popularity. I just care about God's will. I don't care about which way the crowd is going. I just care about how God is moving. I don't care if nobody's on my side. I just want to be on God's side. I'd rather have God in my life than to have the crowd in my life. I'd rather be by myself with God, than be with the crowd and no God."

And I've discovered that even when it looks like I'm by myself, I'm really not by myself. He walks with me. He talks with me. All night and all day

His angels keep watch over me. He promised never to leave me, never to leave me alone!

### He Had Lasting Influence

Noah's high standard of righteous living might have made him an oddball by the low spiritual standards of his day, but God honored him by giving him lasting influence: "But Noah found grace in the eyes of God."

I don't know who Noah's critics were; he outlived his critics. I don't know who his adversaries were; he outlived his adversaries. And all people on whom God has favor have a way of overshadowing their lives and extending their influence beyond their own physical life, and the life span of their critics and adversaries. For they find favor in the eyes of God.

The influence of Martin Luther King Jr. outlasts the evil resistance of Bull Conner, Lester Maddox, George Wallace, and J. Edgar Hoover. He found favor in the eyes of God.

And people may make fun of you, and laugh at you, and ridicule you because you come to church; because you try to serve the Lord; because you have God in your life; because you try to live a holy lifestyle. But the influence of one righteous man who has found favor in the eyes of God will outlast all of the unrighteous souls who criticized you in their day and generation.

Righteous living has lasting influence. Go on and teach Sunday school, and long after you're gone, somebody will remember that you taught them the words of eternal life. Go on and be a scout leader, and some boy will remember that you gave him the tools to make a life and make a difference. Go on and sing your song, and somebody will remember that you inspired them to keep on keeping on. Go on and leave a legacy, and somebody will thank God that you passed this way.

Righteous living has lasting influence. Like the sweet fragrance of expensive perfume, righteous living sweetens up the atmosphere. Like the lingering memory of an unforgettable experience, righteous living leaves a lasting impression. Like the gentle breeze on a warm summer morning righteous living is always refreshing.

People called Noah an oddball, but Noah had lasting influence. He became the link between the generation that was judged and the generation of another chance. We're talking about him now because he had lasting influence. And in these evil days, we need some men who are willing to be God's oddballs. These are the people who make the difference and leave a legacy. These are the people who have lasting influence. People may call you an oddball, but you're God's little oddball.

I'd rather be God's oddball than a self-centered critic of the righteous. I'd rather be God's oddball than the devil's disciple. I'd rather be God's oddball than a big baller and a shot caller in the world.

Jesus was God's oddball. He was so strange that "He came unto His own, and His own received Him not" (John 1:11). He lived an alternative lifestyle. His was the way of the cross. He said, "If any man would come after me, let him deny himself and take up his cross and follow me" (Matthew 16:24). He was content to stand alone. He had to walk that lonesome valley. He had to walk it all by Himself. But He has lasting influence. God raised Him up on Sunday morning with all power in His hand. And now, "If any man will be in Christ, he is a new creation. Old things are passed away and behold all things are become new" (2 Corinthians 5:17).

New thoughts. New ways. New attitude. A new outlook. A new lifestyle. What a wonderful change in my life has been wrought since Jesus came into my heart.

Reclaim...

*Reclaim* means to get back something you possessed previously that was either lost or taken away from you. As Black men, we must own up to the reality that we have lost some of our zeal and zest – as warriors of God. This lost is no real reflection of our inabilities; but is a part of a systemic entanglement of strategies and policies put in place by others. Have you ever unintentionally left a favorite hat somewhere? Or more commonly, how about your cell phone, wallet, favorite pen, or keys? It is troubling when you realize that something you highly value or need to use on a regular basis has been lost, stolen, or misplaced. You are anxious to reclaim that thing that has been taken away from you. So it is with the soul. As men – we must avail our soul for God to reclaim via His spirit, His Word, and His son.

Is it possible to lose the soul? Absolutely! It can be an immediate occurrence or a gradual process. Before you realize it, you have compromised your core values, lost your way in life, or have been lured away by the trappings so prevalent today; desiring short-term pleasure resulting in long-term pain. Social media, pornography, and other such trappings cause people to live dual lives – one way in public life and a whole different person in private life. Yes, losing one's soul begins slowly at first. But in the long run, could lead to devastation of self and others.

The story is told of the frog who is content in a pot of tepid water not realizing it is in a pot that is gradually being heated with fire. The frog has become so comfortable in its warm water that it makes no attempt to jump out of the pot and meets its death because the water continued to heat up and cooked the frog. Fortunately and thanks be to God for the human soul that, through the conscience, can feel the heat, sense the need to get out of it, and choose to be revived, retrieved, and most importantly reclaimed!

How do you *Reclaim* what has been lost? Matthew 16:26, Luke 9:25 and Mark 8:36 ask that question. *"What do you benefit if you gain the whole world and lose your own soul?"* (NLT) What is the question for humankind today? Here it is: "Is it worth it to live beneath my privilege?" The answer must be a resounding "NO! God has something more for us; therefore, you must *Reclaim* your place in the family, in the church, in the community." So begin now, my brother, and *Reclaim* your designated position within your family and this society! It's waiting for you.

Reclaiming the inner man helps bring us closer to God, creating a pathway for restoration. What have we lost? Many men will answer this question differently. However, the answer should center on the love of God. It is important that we reclaim the love of God, and operationalize this in our life. God's love and power are inherently given to us by Him. Reclaiming the love of God equips us with the power of God to accomplish the tasks He has set before us. Oftentimes, instead of leaning on the love and power of God in situations of opposition, or difficult conditions, we allow the enemy to infiltrate our mind, our homes, our relationships, our finances and wreak havoc. Brothers, to *reclaim* what have been taken, we have to acknowledge that we are weak enough to lean on God, and seek his love and guidance. Otherwise, we will remain hostage to our conditions and circumstances, not reclaiming the life that God has predestined. If we're not careful, we will abandon the life God has ordained when we become prisoners to our past, not allowing God to lift us up out of our wretched states. We need to be mindful that a state of hopelessness, a state of despair work to separate us from God's love, and God's promises. We cannot allow this separation and must reclaim the victory that God has over our life. Paul writes to the Romans,

*"Who shall separate us from the love of Christ? Shall persecution famine, or nakedness, or peril, or sword? ..Nay, in all these things we are more than conquerors though him that loves us. For I am persuaded that neither death, nor life, nor angels, nor principalities, nor powers, nor thing present, or things to come, nor height, nor depth, nor any other creature, shall be able to separate us from the love of god, which is in Christ Jesus our Lord"* (Romans 8:33-39).

We must *reclaim* the promises that God have ordered over our life. God has given us His inheritance, and to lay claim to this we must step out on faith and believe God. Being the sons of God we must reclaim our heritage, our legacy, and believe in the promises of God. Keep in mind that reclaiming God's Word removes the fear of the unknown and the oppressor. God has not given us the spirit of fear, *reclaim* your victory.

# How to Stop Our Sisters from Crying

*Kenneth Clayton*

John 11

*According* to the writing and record of John, the beloved disciple, we are delivered to a sad and sorrow-filled moment in the life of a family known to Jesus, in a town called Bethany outside of Jerusalem. This family is not a family in the traditional sense. John gives us no indication of a mother or father alive at the recording of these events. Regardless of their arrangement, they were a family, and as one reads the text closely and carefully, it is discovered that something is wrong. The family is hurting and in pain because an important link in the family unit was dead.

As chapter 11 begins, Jesus and his disciples are somewhere in the villages beyond the Jordan. He is there to preach and teach, bringing glory to God and salvation to those who hear and believes in him. As he engages in ministry in this city and area, Jesus receives word from two sisters, Mary and Martha, that Lazarus, their brother, was sick.

Now we discover in John chapter 11 verse 5 that Jesus loves Mary, Martha, and Lazarus. Scholars suggest that whenever Jesus was in their hometown of Bethany he always made his way to their house. They were an extended part of Jesus' family. In fact, it was Mary who poured costly perfume on Jesus' feet and wiped them with her hair. And because they were so close to him, in the midst of their brother's sickness these two sisters turn to Jesus on behalf of their brother, with the hope that Jesus could make their brother whole and well again.

How many sisters do you know have sat in Mary and Martha's seat? How many mothers in God's house have been where Mary and Martha are in the text, crying over a sick brother and calling on Jesus to make him better?

Brothers, many of us know how Mary and Martha felt. We know what it is to cry about or to cry for a sick brother, a sick son, or a sick grandson. Or, to cry for a brother who is sick on drugs or alcohol; who has low ambition; who makes bad decisions; or who has a heart hardened towards God.

We know how Mary and Martha feel. But inasmuch as we know how they feel, we can learn a lesson from them. Mary and Martha teach us that the only person who can cure a sick brother is Jesus.

Therefore, Mary and Martha sent word to Jesus that their brother, who was Jesus' friend, was sick. And, in so doing, it was their hope and prayer that Jesus would drop everything, come where they were, and heal their brother. But if you keep reading chapter 11, what the sisters expected is not what happened. Not only does Jesus not come quickly, but quite the contrary, he stays where he was for two more days! Then, he announces to his disciples, in verse 7, that it is time to go back to Judea and see about his friend Lazarus!

The disciples are both afraid and confused. They are afraid because when Jesus was in Jerusalem (just two miles outside of Bethany), the Jewish leaders, who did not believe him to be the Messiah, tried to stone him, so Jesus left that city. He and his disciples moved to the other side of Jordan, and while they were away from those hateful people, Jesus receives the news that Lazarus was sick. And, after waiting for two days to pass, Jesus said, "Let's go back."

Back to the place where we were almost killed? Yes.

Back to the place where folk hate us? Yes.

Back to the place where we know our enemy lives? Yes.

Now this makes them afraid, and in addition, they are confused. They are confused because Jesus says, "Lazarus is asleep and I am going back there to wake him up," so the disciples say, "Well, if he's sleeping he will get better." But by verse 14, Jesus clarifies with, "Lazarus is dead!" He further says that he was glad for their sake that the disciples might believe!

And on many of our men's faces around the country on today, this same confusion can be seen. Jesus did not see Lazarus's death as an end. He did not see Lazarus's dying as final, but as a means and an opportunity to display the life-giving, life-altering transformative power of Jesus! The disciples see Lazarus's death as finite, but Jesus saw it as an unfolding opportunity. The disciples see Lazarus's death as a reason to stay where they are, but Jesus sees it as a opportunity to show them who he is and what he is able to do.

Jesus makes his way to Jerusalem. As he is in route, Mary and Martha are surrounded by a company of mourners – men and women who come to comfort them in their time of loss, to offer hope and strength.

Mary and Martha are crying; they are weeping; and they are mourning because their brother is dead. This could be a scene at any house, yours or mine, where sisters are crying over dead brothers.

Now I have been drawn to this text, and have been compelled to focus on this family and on this pivotal moment in their lives, because what Mary and Martha are experiencing in the text is what many a sister, mother, grandmother, wife, daughter – in fact, many a son, brother, father, and grandfather – have also experienced, and perhaps may be experiencing today. Mary and Martha are crying because of the pain they feel, because of the sorrow that fills and invades their lives, because their beloved brother was dead.

Many of us have cried and are crying because our brothers, our fathers, and our sons are dead! Not dead in the physical sense of the word, but dead as it relates to realizing their promise, their potential, and their place with God! There are men who are very much physically alive, but they are in dead situations: dead to alcohol; dead to drugs; dead to incarceration; dead to immorality; dead to unemployment; dead to underemployment.

There are men who are active but dead! There are men reading this book who are breathing, but in reality who are dead! And, because you are dead or are dying, you have caused or are causing the pain of your sisters, your mothers, your children, and your friends who are crying because of you and your dead situation.

There are men who have made decisions that put them on dead-end streets, which have killed their possibilities, killed their potential, and killed their promise. Subsequently you are dead, and somebody is crying for you. Somebody is crying about you. Somebody's tears have your name on them. But, our text offers to those of us who may be dead, and causing pain to our sisters, our mothers, or our children, a way to stop our sisters from crying!

Look at the text again. Jesus is in route to Jerusalem. Martha heard that Jesus was coming and she leaves Mary and the company of mourners and runs to where Jesus is. In verse 21, Martha says, "Lord, if you had been here, my brother would not have died, but I know that even now God will give you whatever you ask."

In the midst of her personal pain, Martha expresses her faith in Christ. Some people read this expression of Martha as an indictment, as if she is saying, "Lord, you should have been here and he would not have died." Either way she is still saying, "Lord, I know you have the power to heal my brother."

And I need to tell somebody else one more time that no matter how sick your situation may be, no matter how dead your situation may be, Jesus can fix it. Jesus can turn it around.

Jesus says to Martha in verse 23, "Your brother will rise again." Martha responds by saying, "I know he will in the resurrection at the last day." Jesus says to her, "I am the Resurrection and the Life. He who believes in me will live even though he dies, and whoever lives and believes in me will never die. Believest thou this?"

A little while later, Mary hears that Jesus is in town and asking for her, and she runs to where he was. She runs to the place where he was with Martha, and she, like Martha, declares her faith in Jesus by saying in verse 32, "Lord, if you were here my brother would not have died." Jesus sees her weeping and watches her fall at his feet in sorrow, and he is moved in his spirit and is troubled. And he asks, "Where have you laid him?"

In verse 38, Jesus arrives at the tomb, and a stone was across the entrance. Jesus says, "Take the stone away." Martha says, "Lord, his body stinks. He has been there four days!" But Jesus tells Martha that she would see the glory of God. The stone was moved away and Jesus prayed to his heavenly Father and says, "Father, I thank you that you have heard me. I know that you always hear me, but I say this for the benefit of those standing here, that they may believe that you sent me." And after he prays in a loud voice he said, "Lazarus, come forth."

Now I must declare that the preachers of another generation were clear and correct as they used their sanctified imagination. They said that it is important that we note that Jesus calls Lazarus by name, for if he not called Lazarus by name, if he would have just said, "Come forth," ALL of the dead from Adam to Lazarus would have gotten up. But he called Lazarus by name and said, "Come forth." And as he does he teaches us how to stop our sisters from crying.

Just like Lazarus, many a black men are dead. You can identify a dead men when:

- He is absent from his family (church, community, college, place of employment). He is dead because he is not where he should be.

- He is in a tomb. Lazarus was dead and in a tomb. He was enclosed, locked in. What tombs are we in?

- He is bound. He is wrapped up. He is tied up and unable to move, love, progress, or praise.

Jesus came to see about Lazarus. Jesus called his name and he did it to prove that only Jesus can turn death into life. Jesus arrived at Lazarus's place of entombment and called Lazarus from death unto life.

Brothers, let me tell you. Jesus is still calling names. He's still calling: dead men to life; sinners to salvation; hopeless men to hope; addicts to accountability; dealers to deliverance; and crooks to Christ. And you can stop sisters from crying if:

- You move the stone that is between you and Jesus. In order for Lazarus to hear the voice of Jesus, the stone had to be rolled away. What is your stone? What is preventing you from hearing Jesus' voice? Whatever it is, move it. If it is guilt, move it. If it is immorality, move it. If it is addiction, move it.

- You listen for his voice. He will call you by your name. And when he calls you, he is calling you to come forth, to come to him, to follow him, to move from death into life. That's what he did for Lazarus and that's what he will do for us.

We can stop our sisters from crying. We can stop our sisters from having pain, from crying about our death, from crying about our plight, from crying about our predicament. If we move the stones that separate us from God; if we hear the voice of Jesus calling our names; if we come forth, we will be called back to life. We will be called into responsibility, into accountability, and the Lord will bless us and use us!

# Raising Dead Men

*Keith Ogden*

Luke 7:11-14

***If you take*** a moment to reflect upon the many issues and concerns plaguing young Black men in today's society, there is likely a burden on your heart about them. As a body of believers, we should focus on their connections to the church and their relationships with the Lord. Ask yourself, are Black men in your life closely connected to the word of God? Are we as excited about the Balm in Gilead as we are about the team that won the NBA Championship? Are we as enthusiastic about leading young Black men to Christ as we are about Lebron James or Steph Curry going into the NBA championship? All of us should feel the gravity of the horror that afflicts young Black men today.

There should be a burden on our hearts because our beautiful Black men of African descent are being pulled out of the church for their lack of knowledge about Jesus Christ, pulled out of the church for sickly half-truths and by the skillful covering up of the other half. I've watched desperately as brother after brother fell for that lie about our names. For some of you have heard that half-truth, which is also a half-lie, and a half-lie is like being half-pregnant—it doesn't make sense.

Some brothers always fall for the familiar lines: "Do you know you have a slave name? Come on over to the Black Man's true religion and we will give you a new name." I want to give you an example of how some of our young Black men are being pulled away from the church.

As a minister of the Gospel and a man who has been ordained by God, I am adamantly opposed to any invasion into the Black churches of America. And I am fully convinced that those of you who are true disciples of the Lord can, with integrity, be about the business of raising dead men, and that's what is happening in this text. Jesus is raising a young man. He is raising a dead man. A man cut off in his prime before he had the chance to live, like so many of our young black men today. Look with me at the text and we can see what lessons are to be learned from it.

There are five distinct issues here that I want us to explore:

- Differentiation
- Confrontation

54

- Liberation
- Transformation
- Restoration

**The first issue is differentiation.** Look at the text: the word differentiates between the committed and the non-committed. Jesus went to a town called Nain (and look who it says is with Jesus: His disciples and a large crowd). Now there is a difference between being a disciple and being among the crowd.

You must understand, my brothers, that everybody who walks with Jesus is not a disciple. Some are just hanging out in the crowd. You see, a disciple tithes; a member of the crowd talks. A disciple is in the word; a member of the crowd is just in the house (in the number). A disciple prays for folks; a member of the crowd talks about folks.

Everybody who is with Christ, everybody who follows Christ, isn't committed to Christ. Matthew 7:21 puts it like this: "Not everyone who says to me, 'Lord, Lord,' shall enter the kingdom of Heaven, but he who does the will of my Father in heaven."

A disciple is committed to follow Jesus, no matter what comes. A crowd member is true to Jesus until something better comes along. You all know what I'm talking about. These people will sit with the Baptist crowd for a minute, with the African Methodist crowd for a minute, with the United Methodist crowd for a minute, with the non-denominational crowd for a minute, and with the Church of God in Christ for a minute. They aren't committed to anybody; they're confused. Everybody following Christ is not in Christ. Some are just in the crowd.

Now, look again at verse 12. Coming from the other direction, there was a man who had died, and he was being carried out. The word says he was his mother's only son, and she was a widow. And notice this, it says, "and with her was a large crowd." One large crowd is following Christ, and another large crowd is following the casket.

Sometimes I'm led to believe that all some churches have on Sunday mornings is a large crowd. The pastors of those congregations might as well have a funeral. And for the most part, that's the only time the church can be filled up, is during a funeral.

And that's what many of our churches are having: funerals, because no ministry is happening, no disciples are committed, there are no programs for the brothers, and no programs for the youth exist. We are boring Jesus.

Some churches every Sunday sound like a broken record: "Yes, he died, yes, he died, just bury him." Our young men are dying in anger and pain, and some are even wondering, "What did I do to drive away my daddy?" Our young Black men and boys are being gunned downed while unarmed in the streets of America. So many of our young Black men and boys are in pain, and some of our young men are following the crowd that leads them away from being fathers and men.

You must understand that a father is an image of a young's man's destiny, a living testimony of what time may bring to pass. A dad should be the first definition of young man's masculinity. More often, however, his absence will leave a young man desperately looking for someone else to "fill in the blank" of his life. If the church doesn't do it, the community will. If the church doesn't do it, the gangs and the drug lords will. If the church doesn't do it, the porn distributors will. If the church doesn't do it, the crack dealers will.

You see, in today's Gospel the crowd isn't interested in what's going on. Look at the crowd following this mother—the people aren't even crying. The mother is the only one weeping. Again, there's a difference between the disciples and the crowd.

There's a stark contrast between membership and discipleship. And you would think that somebody else would be crying when they see a young Black man cut off in his prime. Have you cried about Trayvon Martin? Have you cried about John Crawford, who was gunned down because he held a pellet gun in his hands? Somebody ought to be crying.

I don't know about you, but I can't stand to see and read about or preach the funerals of young Black men robbed of their potential because of the color of their skin; cut down because of cars, or because of jewelry or because of gangs and a code of ethics. And during funerals, some young Black men in attendance won't even cry. They appear hard and cold. They will stand there at the coffin and say, "Man, this stuff is messed up. You see homie gone. Somebody is going to have to pay for this." I can't stand it, because the young Black men, like the deceased young man's mother and sister, should be crying.

Jonathan Capehart of the *Washington Post* reported that Levar Jones was pulled over for a seatbelt violation by now-former South Carolina state trooper Sean Groubert on September 4. He said, and I quote, "Thanks to the startling and graphic dashcam video we get to see every African American's worst nightmare unfold in seconds." A request to see a driver's license followed by an attempt to comply leads to Jones being shot by someone who, as *The Post's* Radley Balko correctly says, "should never be a police officer again."

You see, a life full of promise is cut off. Somebody ought to be pierced by the pathology of a mismanaged promise. And if that doesn't make you cry, I don't know what will. The hard, cold facade that some young men portray isn't African. Somewhere along the way, we've gotten lost and confused. People in West Africa have a way of greeting each other. If you asked them how they are doing, the response is: "If your day was well, then my day was well." In other words, how I'm doing is just important as how you are doing. Until all of us are free, none of us are free. My friend, the Reverend Darryl Sims, in his book, ***Adam Come Home*** says, and I quote, *the Black man can only be free when his mind is free*.

But you see, the crowd could care less; they are just spectators and they are there just to see the show. There is no emotional involvement and no spiritual involvement anywhere in the scene before us in Luke 7.

So the word *differentiate* characterizes those who are disciples and those who belong in the crowd.

**The second issue is confrontation.** We are always confronting somebody—we are confrontational people. But Jesus is moved by what He sees. The word says He had compassion and was touched by the woman's tears. Many of us, especially men, have this crying thing mixed up. Brothers always walk around talking about "be strong." You can be strong all you like, but if you're not willing to shed a tear here and there— the internal meltdown can cause you a great deal of health problems.

You see, you cry because you are strong. You cry because you care. You cry because you have compassion, because what you are witnessing matters to you. When Jesus sees something that matters to Him, He acts on our behalf. He confronted the situation in Luke 7.

The word says He walked over and touched the casket. You see, when you try to raise somebody from the dead, don't expect them to come to you! Dead folk will not come to you; you have to walk over to where they are. I don't care how pretty your church is or about its reputation. I don't care how much it costs or whether the mortgage was burned years ago. I don't care how many people it will seat. It doesn't matter how much or how pretty your carpet is. You better get up and go to where the dead folks are. You have to go to them and confront their seemingly lifeless situation.

The word says that Jesus touched the coffin. (Read Numbers 19:11-16.) Jesus was not supposed to have any contact with the dead. He was a holy man, a rabbi. He knew that if He touched the body of a dead person, he would have to be unclean for seven days. But you see, real ministry happens when you step into the place where the need to be healed and even brought back to life exists. And that's confrontation. In other words, if you want to raise dead men, you've got to touch some folks you're not supposed to touch.

I remember when I was in Tacoma, Washington, and there was an AIDS Awareness Sunday at most of the Black churches. Many people were uninvolved, as if to say: "AIDS doesn't affect us. We're saved, sanctified, and . . . full of ignorance." AIDS ministry means touching folks you're not supposed to touch. Alcohol ministry means touching folks you're not supposed to touch—and that means confrontation!

Look! Jesus dealt first with the coffin carriers.

In our funeral services, we have family members and loved ones who serve as pallbearers. In Jesus' culture, these were professional people who carried out this task. Do you remember that restriction about touching the dead? The coffin carriers were the ones who did this as their profession, which means they were always unclean. They carried bodies back and forth because they had a vested interest in lifting the dead. You must understand, we have professional people who also have a vested interest in our young Black men being dead.

There are some people who have a vested interest in your death. Dope dealers are coffin carriers. Gang members are coffin carriers. Gun runners are coffin carriers. Gun dealers are coffin carriers. Prisons and prisons builders are coffin carriers.

Notice that Jesus doesn't call the young man a lad or a boy; that means he was past the bar mitzvah age; he was in his teens, a teenager. His mother had no man in her life and in Northeast Africa, no man in the home often times meant that, this loss, or absence, undermined both the future of the family and of the community.

When we lose young brothers to drugs, or to the criminal justice system or to the morticians, this lack of productivity undermines the future of the entire Black community. And Jesus confronts the situation head-on. Watch Jesus now! He made contact with the context that affected the life of this young man. "He touched the coffin; and the word says the coffin carriers stopped. "They stood still." Sometimes before you can raise the dead, you have to stop the people carrying the coffin. You have to stop the professionals who make a living off other folk dying. And if you look closer at the text, it says he reached out and touched the coffin—in other words, he stopped them with an action. You see, you can't preach to the coffin carriers. No, no, no. You got to confront them with a concrete act. Jesus stopped the funeral procession!

**The third issue we see in the text is liberation.** Jesus sets the young man free. Look at Him: He says, "Young man." All of us who follow Jesus have to learn to be about the business of calling folks by the right name. You remember when Jesus raised Lazarus from the dead. You remember all the names they called him over in John the 11th chapter. They called him dead, they called him stinky, they called him decomposed, they called him beyond help. But you remember what Jesus called him: "Lazarus."

Before you can get folk to act right, you got to name them right. Look at the text again. Jesus said, "Young man" – not homie. Young Man – not bro. Young man – not Junebug. Young man – not baby brother. Young man – not gangbanger. And Jesus says, "Rise; get up; you don't belong to death; you belong to me." He says, "Get up! Your people built pyramids; stop talking about what you can't do. Get up! Get off welfare. Get up! Stop abusing alcohol. Get up! Get off your do-nothing stool. Get a job. Go back to school. Get up!" Then Jesus sets him free; Jesus liberates him.

**The fourth issue is transformation.** To transform means to change. Look at the text: the young man began to do what dead folks aren't supposed to do. First, he sat up (transformation). Dead folks don't sit up; but when you hear the voice of Jesus, I declare, it will get you up. He'll raise you from a dead place when you hear His voice. Not only did the young man sit up, he also began to speak; I believe he said something.

You must understand my brothers and my sisters, that when the Lord gets you up, you ought to say something. When the Lord gets you up, you ought to praise Him. When the Lord gets you up, you ought to tell somebody. When the Lord gets you up, you ought to shout "Hallelujah!" When the Lord gets you up, say, "What a mighty God we serve!" and then thank Him, and praise His Holy name. Let the world know that the Lord raised you; the Lord, saved you; He turned your life around; He gave you your sanity. Testify that the Lord has been mighty good to you.

Luke says, "So he who was dead sat up and began to speak" (NKJV), and he probably said:

> Shackled by a heavy burden,
> 'Neath a load of guilt and shame;
> Then the hand of Jesus touched me,
> And now I am no longer the same.
> He touched me,
> O, He touched me,
> and O, the joy that floods my soul;
> Something happened, and now I know,
> He touched me and made me whole.[1]

That's the celebration! But before you can get to celebration, there is restoration.

**The fifth issue is restoration.** Jesus gave the young man back to his mother. Jesus restored him to his rightful place in the community.

You see, my brothers, when the Lord gets you up, He's going to send you back to where you died. And that's restoration. He gave him back to his mother.

When God gets you up, He wants you to examine your own life. And He doesn't leave the sisters behind. Men, speak up for the women in your lives. Stand up for them. Stop fighting them and just love on them. God is in the business of restoration. He puts broken lives back together again. God puts broken people back together again. "God will restore you to the wholeness he had in mind; when he first made you.

For I heard the voice of Jesus say, "Come unto me, all ye that labour and are heavy laden, and I will give you rest. Take my yoke upon you, and learn of me; for I am meek and lowly in heart: and ye shall find rest unto your souls. For my yoke is easy, and my burden is light" (Matthew 11:28-30, KJV).

You may be experiencing a spiritual death of some kind, but remember that God raises dead men! If you really want to resurrect your dead situation, just believe in God's resurrection power. Believe by faith and stand up and command your situation. Rise!

Go find your son in that tomb of drugs! Raise your drunken father from the gutter of the city street! Don't give up; don't give in. God is still in the restoring business. He will raise you; He will raise you; He will give you a new life, a new heart, and a new attitude. Yes, He will. Restoring dead men . . . God is still in the business of restoring lives. Don't turn your back on Him; don't walk away. It may get rough sometimes, but hold on to God's unchanging hand!

Can I tell about Jesus? He died a brutal death. He was betrayed by a friend. He was bounced around within the court system. He was hung out before his family and friends. He died! However, on the third day, He got up with all power in His hands!

Notes

1.    William J. Gaither, "He Touched Me."
2.    John Newton, "Amazing Grace," stanza 1.
3.    "Amazing Grace," stanza 4 attributed to John Rees.

# When Your Change Starts Making Sense

*Tyrone P. Jones IV*

Luke 15:11-20

*My Brothers*, I have to tell you that we live in a senseless society. It seems to me that more importance is being put on things that don't really matter. We seem to be majoring on the minor things and minoring on the major things. Just this week, I saw people lined up in masses for a pair of Nike Galaxy Foam Posit Sneakers that glow in the dark. One hundred police officers were called in to police inner city youth for buying these $200.00-a-pair so-called "dope-dealer shoes." But check this out – the kids don't want to wear them—they want to resell them or collect them. That's why it is important that we give positive reinforcements to our children to let them know that sneakers don't make you! Just remember that Jesus will not forsake you! There is a need for some change in order for life to start making sense!

There's a story of a man who was locked up in an insane asylum because he lost his sense of reality. The man one day was looking outside of his barred window, and he saw a man pull over across the street from the insane asylum with a flat tire. The man stopped to change the tire, and after he took off the lugs nuts from the flat tire, they all fell into the storm drain and could not be recovered. The man was frantic; he started pacing back and forth. The man in the insane asylum yelled out to him to just take one lug nut from each of the other three tires and use that with the spare, and if he drives slowly, he could make it to a garage about two miles down the road. The man outside followed the recommendation and said thanks, but then he was puzzled because this advice came from a man who was in an insane asylum. The man outside asked the man inside the asylum, "If you knew how to think like this then why are you locked up in there?" And the man on the inside responded, "I may not have any sense, but I am not stupid!"

In our text, verse 17 says, "when he came to his senses" (NIV). Or "when he came to himself" (KJV). This means at some point he was lost from himself in order to come to himself. Or (NIV) he was lost from his senses, when he came to his senses.

The entire 15th chapter of Luke is a trilogy, three stories that define the attitude of God. What's important to notice is that the Pharisees and teachers of the law were offended that Jesus was packing the church out with tax collectors and sinners, and they questioned among themselves the validity of Jesus' ministry because this was not making any sense to them. But get this, they didn't understand the attitude of God toward those who were lost. So then Jesus gives three parables/stories to help them understand. The first story is about a lost sheep that the shepherd goes after and finds. That's the attitude of God. The second story talks about a woman who lost one of her silver coins, but when she sweeps the house and looks carefully she finds what she was looking for. That is the attitude of God. When God receives the lost, God rejoices.

In the final story, there is a father who had two sons. The father is representative of the attitude of God toward those who are lost. Now the younger son comes to the father and says, "Give me my portion of my inheritance now!" Right here is how we can tell that this young man has given in to some senseless things. Listen to his request and listen to his conversation: "Give me my share of the estate!" This is senseless because everybody knows that you don't get an inheritance until the father dies and is no longer around. This request shows that this young man has gotten too big for his britches. He has a get-rich-and-die spending mentality! No wonder he didn't have anything in the end because all he did was spend! He would have been the type of brother who was always in the lottery line playing the number hoping for a big score! He would have been the type of brother who would have gotten caught up in one of those pyramid schemes trying to get rich. He didn't understand what it meant to work hard and save your money. He tried to start off where other people have left off!

The son's request is also senseless because he is claiming stuff that doesn't belong to him. "Give me mine now! Give me my stuff now!" The stuff doesn't belong to him, but it belongs to his father. We have to be careful claiming stuff that doesn't belong to us because, guess what, even if you possess it doesn't mean that you own it! Because if you lease, rent, charge, or have a consumer loan to get it, it doesn't mean you own it. (Say amen!) Even in the kingdom of God we have to be careful talking about what belongs to us: "This is my church, that my pew, that's my seat, that's my money . . ." Oh, no – you need to read what it says in Psalm 24: "The earth is the Lord's and the fullness thereof . . ."

We need to understand that what we have is ours by stewardship and it is God's by ownership! And although God owns it, we should thank God He lets us manage it!

Watch this! The text says that the father divided his property between them. This lets me know that although the father divided the sons' inheritance, what he gave the son still belonged to the father. In Jewish custom the inheritance of the father doesn't go to the youngest son, but it is given to the eldest son to divide amongst his siblings. But this young son felt a sense of entitlement! That is what is senseless. I tell my children what my father and mother told me. They said to me and my brother that in this world nobody owes you anything! We are not entitled to anything! Even if you got good grades, and even if you were a model student, if you are grown and are going out on your own nobody owes you anything! Because you can't live off someone else's labor.

This young man was exhibiting senseless behavior. Some people will say, "Well, pastor, the economy is bad, so I want to help them out." OK, but understand that if you are unemployed then it's your responsibility to look for employment until you get a job! And if you have a job that you don't like, you have to learn to work the job you have until you get the job that you really want! Stop living off somebody else's labor! This just doesn't make any sense!

I was driving downtown in Bridgeport and I parked at a meter and fed the meter some money, but the meter didn't work. So I thought if I kept feeding the meter that the meter was going to work. Then I got a parking enforcement officer and I told her what happened, and she told me that I needed to stop feeding the meter and that she would put up an "out of order" sign on the meter that says it isn't working. If people are grown but keep asking for money, stop feeding the meter and just tell them that they are out of order. Senseless behavior!

Brothers, can I show you something else in the text? As soon as the son received what he thought he was entitled to from the father, he left the father's house and distanced himself from the father. Senseless behavior! Now I understand why God can't bless us with too much because when we had a little bit of something we stayed in the father's house and we were connected to the father. But the moment we get a big blessing, or what we think we need, that's when we run from the father's house. When you had one suit in the closet you were at church; now you have a walk-in closet full of clothes but you say you have nothing to wear. When you drove your Toyota Tercel you laid hands on it and prayed in order to get to church, but now that you got an upgrade you lay hands on Sunday, not to pray, but to wash your ride. Senseless behavior! The son's rebellious behavior was against God who is the father who supplied what he needed.

The younger son got the money, and the Bible says he squandered his wealth in wild living and prostitutes. Senseless behavior! I want this time of fasting and prayer to hit home for us, because where our treasure is there our heart is also. This is the time to reevaluate our current living conditions. We need to look at what we do with what we have!

He spent his wealth on prostitutes. A prostitute is somebody who sells what they are supposed to give in love. Brothers, stop getting involved with people who only want you for what they can get from you. Make sure you find somebody who wants to be with you not for what you have, but because of who you are. When the son's money ran out, his friends ran out. When you're making it rain with dollars everybody is your friend, but when you are in pain and hollering only a true friend stays by your side.

He was doing a job that went against his culture, customs, and beliefs. Sin will drive you to work in unclean places and around unclean things and to contemplate unclean ideas. Sin will make you crazy! It will make go further than you wanted to go, doing stuff that you never thought you would do! Sin will have you stay longer than you really wanted to stay. Sin will have you pay more than you wanted to pay, because there is a cost to the insanity of sin.

But here's the good news: it's in this situation that a metamorphosis of the mind took place, and sense replaced senselessness. The son repented! Repentance is the changing of one's mind, and when you change your mind you automatically change your ways. He took a hard look at himself in his situation and said, "My father's employees live better than this. I have sinned against my father and I have sinned against God. I am no longer worthy to be called my father's son. I am going to ask him to make me like one of his hired men." He says, "*Make* me . . ." In senseless days he said, "*Give* me . . ." That ought to shout you right there! Some of us need to go back to the father and instead of asking him to give you everything, you need to ask him to make you into what he wants you to be.

When you come to your senses, you will run to the father's house. There is love in the father's house. There is joy in the father's house. There is salvation in the father's house. There is deliverance in the father's house. When you come to your senses and get to the father's house, the father can release some stuff into your life. And the good news is the father gave the son stuff like he had never left home. Forgiveness would have been enough. Access back home would have been enough. But God says, "No, go get my boy a robe. Go get my boy a ring. Go get him shoes for his feet. Let's have some lamb chops and let's party like its 1999."

Aren't you glad of this reality: after one repents – there's a God who can give you another chance? Watch this! What the son was looking for in the far country, the text lets us know he could have gotten right in the father's house. All of the clothes, shoes, a party, joy, a health relationship, a family, money, whatever he needed were not in the world but right here in the church. Give me the church verses the club any day!

Once you repent of your sins and change your mind, that's when your change will start making sense. That's when God will release some stuff that was already there for you. It's about repentance if you want what he is about to release.

I heard a preacher tell a story about being lost in a small town where he was scheduled to preach. The GPS was not working, but he saw some men standing on the corner. The preacher asked for directions to the church. The people said, "You are going in the wrong direction. You need to make a U-turn and then go right. Once you go right, then you go up the hill and up the hill you will see a cross. Just follow the cross until you get to the church."

Brothers, I'm writing to tell you that if you are going in the wrong direction, you need to make a U-turn. Once you make that U-turn, go right. Once you go right, then just look for the cross, and then follow the cross until you get to the father's house! Brothers, remember you ought to praise the Lord for U-turns, praise the Lord for going in the right direction, praise the Lord and just follow the cross until you get to the father's house.

# Can You Be Trusted with a Changed Man?

*Derek Triplett*

Acts 9:10-19

*When* you look at the prefix of the words that dominate the verbiage of Christianity, it becomes clear that we, the church of the Lord Jesus, are in the business of change. Words like repent, redeem, redemption, reconcile, reclaim, reform, repair, renewed, and remake give the clear indication that something had to be done over.

The prefix "re," meaning again, makes it clear that the work of God in our lives is at the very least a second work. Although we are, as Scripture says, fearfully and wonderfully made, we are simultaneously born in sin and shaped in iniquity from the womb because of original sin transferred to us from Adam and Eve. Whoever and whatever we are in Christ at this point is because God has either changed us or given us the freedom, power, and opportunity to make personal changes ourselves. Much if not most of the good and godly traits and character that we have is not because we were ready made. It is because we have been made over, and he's still working on us.

Part of the responsibility and seemingly the challenge of the faith community and the portions of the world at large is that we struggle to get over what we have seen, heard about, experienced, or been a victim of in the life of someone who has been made over. Sin leaves a crimson stain. Jesus washes and sanitizes all of our imperfections. Sin, failure, wrongdoing, and mistakes have the potential to leave a constant stigma that we have a problem letting go. A negative stigma can box you in and get you left out. It can hinder your efforts and block your progress. There are those who are marginalized, disenfranchised, vilified, and unjustly scrutinized because they have been stigmatized, and probably none more than the urban male.

Felon, Pimp, Dead-beat dad, Dog, Thug, Hustler, Buster, Trifling, No good N-word, and if the sentence starts with the words "he ain't" what usually follows is a word that starts with "s," ends with "t," and has "hi" in the middle. Now unfortunately all of these negative labels are true in many cases. Black men are committing crimes at an alarming rate. Sure there are many contributing factors to the concrete jungles of inner city where "kill or be killed" and "get or get got" are the rules of the street. Nevertheless our communities are not safe. And yes, we have to protect black males from the cops, but we also have to protect ourselves from many black males. Many black fathers are reckless and irresponsible. When I ask young urban males, "What is the first thing that comes to mind when I say 'father'?" most of the time the answer is, "absent."

The maltreatment of women by us is well-documented. There are so many hit-it-and-quit-it men that leave a trail of broken women in their path. The reported cases of physical and sexual abuse are numerous, and we cannot count what goes unreported. Too many black males won't go to school, choose not excel while in school, and won't go to work. It's all true. It goes on and on. But what happens when a man comes to himself and God makes him over? What happens when what a man is notorious for being becomes what he used to be? What happens when he changes? What are his prospects? How will he be accepted by his friends, family, and even the church? Can a changed man find a safe place to grow among the Christians? How will you receive and relate to him? Can you be trusted with a changed man?

In the text, Saul of Tarsus has just experienced conversion. Prior to conversion Saul was a murderer. He had people killed. He had Christian men and women dragged out of the church. The chief priests had given him the responsibility to do what he was doing. He sought to eliminate anyone who called on the name of Jesus. He was a very dangerous man. He was brilliant, passionate, powerful, and wrong. What a potentially lethal combination. It made him a deadly individual known and feared by many. But on the Damascus road, Jesus saved him. Saul, the terror from Tarsus, is redeemed and reborn. Jesus changes him. God now has to trust Paul to a human's care.

After people receive Jesus they need some other *people* who serve Jesus. Salvation places us into the body of Christ. Jesus is the head of the church, and Jesus is not solely all that the radically redeemed need. When a person comes to Christ, they need the assistance, care, and camaraderie of other members of the body. God decides to trust Paul to Ananias.

The Lord called to him in a vision, "Ananias!"

"Yes, Lord," he answered.

The Lord told him, "Go to the house of Judas on Straight Street and ask for a man from Tarsus named Saul, for he is praying. In a vision he has seen a man named Ananias come and place his hands on him to restore his sight."

God says to Ananias:

- Engage him
- Embrace him
- Empower him
- Endorse him

### Engage Him

Ananias hears God but wants nothing to do with Saul. "Lord," Ananias answered, "I have heard many reports about this man and all the harm he has done to your saints in Jerusalem. And he has come here with authority from the chief priests to arrest all who call on your name."

Ananias fears Saul. Saul's reputation precedes him. God now tells Ananias to go find a man he would rather hide from. Ananias's ministry assignment makes him fear for his life, and yet, God is requiring him to seek after Saul and engage him. To be willing to engage Paul, Ananias must get past what he believes he knows about Paul's past. In the case of Paul, it is his immediate past; it's been only three days.

The question on the table is this: Are you willing to have something to do with a brother you previously wanted nothing to do with? Are you willing to engage the ex-hustler, murderer, homosexual, dead-beat dad, or ex-thief whom Jesus saves? I am not speaking of just the ones whose past is semi-private. Can God trust you to engage the ones everybody knows?

Let's revisit Ananias's fear. How does he overcome it? Well, loving Saul is a start, for perfect love casts out fear. Secondly, he must have real faith in the redemptive power of Jesus Christ. God's love can penetrate the darkest heart. His grace can reach the worst sinner. God's power can change the most wicked person, and we who have already received his love and grace must always believe that God can redeem, renew, regenerate, and restore. To the utmost Jesus saves.

### *Embrace Him*

When we think of embrace we think of a hug. Everyone loves a warm embrace. Yet, conceptually embrace means to receive to one's self. It means to accept. I've learned that relative to hugs, people can give you cold embraces. Everyone who hugs you doesn't accept you. God says to Ananias, "Accept Saul. I know what he's done but accept him. You know his reputation but accept him, embrace him. Embrace him for I have enlisted him." The Lord said to Ananias, "Go! This man is my chosen instrument."

Paul is now saved and delivered for the safety of the church. He is reborn in order to benefit the church. Saul the "ex" would become Paul the "next." God chose him. He chose him as a matter of prerogative. God can choose whomever he chooses. In our eyes they may not be worthy but God's choice does not require our approval. He is sovereign. It is his prerogative. And as always God makes the right choice. That fact must be trusted when the choice is made. It is easy for us to look in hindsight. We see what Paul accomplished for the cause of Christ. We know his commitment, sacrifice, and success. Yet, Ananias only knows that God has chosen him. That has to be enough to start the journey.

When God makes a choice we must trust God even if we don't trust the chosen. I remember when I was called to my first church. I was 23. I was not the choice of the search committee, the music ministry, and others, but I was God's choice and the choice of the majority of the voting members. A powerful lady in the church came to me a few weeks prior to the final vote and said to me, "I don't want you to be our pastor but it's obvious that is what God wants and what is going to happen. I just want you to know that I won't fight you." She was willing to take the journey even though she did not approve of the choice.

When God chooses someone we do not want to embrace we should do as this woman did and even more. The new in Christ regardless of their past need us. The changed man needs us. Saul needed Ananias. The sovereign God said, "I have enlisted him, and I need you, Ananias, to warmly embrace him." Don't be frozen toward whom God has chosen.

## Empower Him

God says to Ananias, "Lay hands on him; I could have done it but you do it." It is an amazing honor that God allows us to be vessels and channels of his power. We are able to be God's hands as he empowers others. It is the ministry of impartation. Why does God use Ananias? He is purging him from his own prejudice and training him to see a transformed person through the right lens. God wanted Ananias to know that he can change anyone. God wanted Ananias to know that he could call anyone.

But this is primarily a ministry to Saul and more than just a message to Ananias. God wanted Saul to know that he works through people. God wanted him to know that he is accepted.

Can God trust you and your church with a changed man? If so empower him. Place your hands on him. Give him his vision back. Help him get out of a position of dependency and helplessness. God has work for him to do.

## Endorse Him

Baptism was a public endorsement. Ananias was called to endorse Saul, not embarrass him.

> Then Ananias went to the house and entered it. Placing his hands on Saul, he said, "Brother Saul, the Lord – Jesus, who appeared to you on the road as you were coming here – has sent me so that you may see again and be filled with the Holy Spirit." Immediately, something like scales fell from Saul's eyes, and he could see again. He got up and was baptized.

There are people whom others are embarrassed to be connected with because the stigma that they carry. You don't want to be stained by their stigma. But God needs some people to endorse brothers he has changed. When people ask you, "Do you know that he was this or that?" you should say, "Yes, I know. But you should see what God is doing with him now!"

Someone needs your endorsement. Like the father has endorsed you, do it for someone else. Be trusted with a changed man.

# He Asked For A Hand-Out But Got A Hand-Up

*Raynard Smith*

Acts 3:1-10

*According* to the text, for over forty years (Acts 4:22) this man had suffered from an ailment which rendered him lame. He was born that way (3:2). He had never known the freedom of going anywhere without having to rely on others to carry him there. He was totally dependent upon the goodwill of others, be it family members, friends, and sometimes maybe even strangers. He could not do for himself. He could not work a job. We are not told whether he had a family or not, whether he was married or not; all we know is that this man is an invalid in need of others to support him in getting to the gate where he is relegated to begging for alms.

It would seem that this man had been a beggar for many, if not most, of those forty-plus years. It may be that he had staked out a certain "territory" at the temple. At least we know that for some time this man was carried daily to the gate of the temple, a gate identified here as the "Beautiful" gate located on the east side of the temple. It seems that the gate was this lame beggar's station, much as a newspaper carrier would find a suitable location and return there day after day, or like a fisherman who returns to the same spot to fish time and again because it has yielded him good success in the abundance of fish. Experience will tell you to return to the same spot when you find a good spot that yields great results. Some might even venture to call it "my lucky spot." It brings about good results. This man no doubt had his favorite spot and a certain time to be there.

Now in reference to the lame man, we are not told what this man had heard about Jesus or whether he had ever tried to reach Jesus so that he could be healed during Jesus' time of ministry. It would seem that the man would have given considerable thought to Jesus during those times when Jesus visited Jerusalem and especially that final week of Jesus' public ministry, before His death. This was a week characterized by daily appearances in the temple for teaching and also for healing.

Matthew 21:14-16 tells us: "And the blind and the lame came to Jesus in the temple, and Jesus healed them. But when the chief priests and the scribes saw the wonderful things that Jesus had done, and the children who were crying out in the temple and saying, 'Hosanna to the Son of David,' they became indignant, and said to Him, 'Do you hear what these are saying?' And Jesus said to them, 'Yes; have you never read, 'Out of the mouth of infants and nursing babes thou has prepared praise for thyself'?"

Is it possible that this man had made efforts to reach Jesus to be healed? The problem was that he was immobilized by his ailment. Men carried him to the temple to beg each day. There they would leave him. Then in the evening (it would seem) they would carry him back home. Perhaps Jesus passed by this lame man from a distance, but the lame man was unable to press through the crowds or to call out loudly enough to be heard above the crowds by the Master. It sounds something like a "Catch 22" situation to me. The man needed to be healed, and Jesus could heal him, but he had to get to Jesus in order to be healed, and his inability to walk on his own prevented him from getting there, not unlike the situation described in John 5:1-9, where we see Jesus healing the lame man at the pool of Bethzatha after asking him, "Do you want to be made well?"

It is not altogether clear whose faith it was primarily that was instrumental in this man's healing – was it Peter's and John's or the lame man's or a combination of all? – but it would seem that this man had some measure of faith (cf. 3:16). Could it be that this man had hoped Jesus would heal him, but just could not get to Him? How this man's hopes of healing must have been crushed when Jesus was led outside the city to that cross! And yet, after the death of Jesus, it was Jesus who had healed him. Let us see how it came to pass.

It was the ninth hour (the "third hour" in Acts 2:15), which would have been 3:00 p.m. Peter and John were on their way to the temple to observe a regular time of prayer and offering of sacrifice (17). As they were heading toward or into the temple, the lame man was being carried to his normal post, at the "Beautiful" gate. He was not, as we so often visualize him, sitting or lying down at the gate, but only on his way. He had not quite gotten to his station yet when he spotted Peter and John and decided to strike out as he had done so often to beg for monetary support, which was his life sustenance. As he was approaching his station, he observed these two men nearby about to go into the temple.

Beggars generally seem to get attention by calling out to those who would pass by. Almost instinctively, I think, this man called out with his usual petition. Here were two prospects. He might as well get right at his task. How convenient it was that this lame man decided to have himself planted right by the gate Beautiful at the time that pious worshippers would be making their way for service. These were people who were accustomed to fulfilling their religious obligation of alms-giving. It was a sure strategy to guarantee that the lame man's begging would not go unheard or unrewarded, for at three o'clock in the afternoon those headed for evening prayer would be most inclined to give alms to the poor. This lame man had it all figured out. All he was looking for was a hand-out as he had done so many times, a hand-out that would last him until the next time he needed to come back and resume his begging.

I am not certain we can understand this account apart from having experienced a beggar or two. I am sure you have been approached by someone who came up to you and asked you to help him by giving him some money. He made known to you his need hoping to appeal to your heart of compassion for pity upon his circumstance. Some have approached us with a genuine need – they were truly hungry and had no money or food to eat. Others have approached us with a tale as long as the day; perhaps it was not genuine and may have been a request for money to supply their addiction to drugs or alcohol. However, they made known to us their need in hopes that we would respond affirmatively.

When I went with my family to Los Angeles, I saw a large number of beggars – these were people who were homeless. They were living outdoors on what is called *skid row*. They had no place to go. They had no money, no fresh clothes, no means of refreshing themselves. They spent most of their day trying to think of ways to survive, even if it meant stealing. Oh, how I thought about their plight – many of them were afflicted by addictions to drugs and alcohol and mental illness. They needed help that required something more than money could provide for them. They needed deliverance from substance abuse that had so entangled their lives. They needed restoration to their right minds. In many respects they were not unlike this beggar lying at the gate Beautiful.

I am told by my friend Joseph, who is from India, that in India there are so many beggars that there is no way one could respond to all of them. The solution was often not to "see" any of them, to ignore them. But the beggars made this difficult. Those who were mobile would press themselves on you. They would approach your taxi at an intersection, tugging at your sleeve and pleading for help. Those not mobile would call out for charity. The beggar would be aggressive, something like the salesmen as you try to walk through the appliance stores or the car salesman at the car dealership. You would concentrate on not seeing them as they converged on you, and you hurried to get through the section before you were trapped.

In this instance, the roles appear somewhat reversed. The beggar called out all right, but he doesn't seem to expect anything to happen. After all, he has not yet reached his station, and they are nearly out of his territory. I think the beggar hardly looked up, for he simply expected to be ignored or he might have been ashamed. Had he been directly in front of them, perhaps he would have stood a chance, but not here. Yet it appears that whatever the beggar did somehow he got the attention of Peter and John. I'd like to think that they were moved with compassion.

Peter and John did not respond typically, however. It was not the beggar who fixed his eyes on Peter and John, but they who first fixed their eyes on him. He may not have expected anything from them, but they fully intended to do something for him. It is noteworthy that Peter and John had no money to give him. Surely it was not that they were opposed to giving to the poor, but they could not give what they did not possess. They had no money. It may have been that what little they had they gave it into the common pool to be distributed to all according to their needs. But they did give what they had. How fortunate for the beggar. The best he hoped for was a little money — a hand-out. He did not get money, but he did receive his health and mobility — a hand-up. He asked for a hand-out but got a hand-up.

Who are the lame of our day in our social and cultural context? Who are the lame in need of a hand-up? My brothers, the lame within our social context are our brothers upon who has been foisted a negative identity because of poverty, racism, narcotics/drug addictions, and unemployment. These social conditions have resulted in many of our black and brown youth/men being incarcerated. 27.2% of our brothers and sisters live in poverty. Many are underemployed or unemployed. Many are locked out of obtaining a job due to the fact that they failed to complete high school.

Young Black males across the board score below their counterparts in other racial and ethnic groups when it comes to graduation rates, literacy rates, and college preparedness. And many African American men, in turn, are virtually locked out of employment and are filling up the nation's prisons in disproportionate numbers.

The majority of the 2.3 million people incarcerated in U.S. prisons and jails are people of color, people with mental health issues and drug addiction, people with low levels of educational attainment, and people with a history of unemployment or underemployment. But no matter how dismal the statistics on Black America may be, there still is hope. There is a God who sits high and looks low and who sees and knows the plight of His people. This God is available and willing to give us a hand-up. God moves through human history and makes God's concern for the plight of the poor known. This is the same God who told a young Israel as a people, "When you harvest the grain I want you to leave one tenth of the field standing, don't harvest it all; leave one-tenth standing for the widows, wayfarers, and orphans. Leave some of your grain for those who are dispossessed, homeless, and those who have no means of their own to make their way in life."

God has always been concerned about the poor, the dispossessed, and the marginalized. And today through you and me God wants to make Godself known to those who feel that they have been left out, those who might have feelings of despair and feel that they have been forgotten by America and even by God. God wants to use us to reach those who are just like this lame man—ostracized and counted out. God wants to use us to give people a hand-up.

A hand-up on the macro scale is the Affordable Health Care Act, which has secured access to medical assistance for millions who were at one time locked out. A hand-up is the initiative to raise the minimum wage to $10.10, which would guarantee that each full-time person would earn a wage that would put them above the poverty level. A hand-up on the micro level is to engage in mentoring relationships with young black males who have had the misfortunate of not being raised with a father in the home to provide them with the kind of values that only a man can share with his son and even daughter. Mentors give young boys and girls a hand-up by providing them with supervision, love, and guidance (affection, attention, correction, and direction). A hand-up is to provide tutoring and support for those who for whatever reason struggle with learning and are thinking of dropping out or those who did not stay in school long enough to get their high-school diploma and now find themselves locked out of an ever-demanding job market.

A hand-up is to demonstrate the love of Jesus, showing that you care about the plight of the poor, the marginalized, and the dispossessed. You are not just content in talking about it, but you put your efforts into bringing about a remedy however small. Yes, you and I can make a significant difference in the lives of a young person who may have had a rough start. A hand-up is to advocate that there be drug treatment and alcohol treatment centers available for those who have become entangled in the web of drug or alcohol addiction. A hand-up is what people need and how the church should respond.

Let us commit ourselves to living a life that extends the right hand of love, concern, and fellowship to lift our brothers who may have fallen by the wayside. They are the lame today and feel that they are being counted out, but they are not forgotten. God loves them and wants to give them a hand-up. And the reason why I know this is because I am reminded of God giving us the greatest hand-up that has ever been extended. It is recorded in John 3:16: "For God so loved the world, that God gave His only begotten Son, that whosoever believeth in him should not perish but have everlasting life." When Jesus gave His life on the cross for your sins and mine, for the black, the brown, the red, and white woman and man, when He gave His life, He gave us the greatest hand-up the world will ever know.

Peter seems to know from the outset (and John too) what he was going to do for this man. Somehow he knew that he had the power to heal this man, and also that it was God's will for him to do so. After all, he and the other followers had just been endowed with a power from on high – The Holy Spirit. Yes, they spoke in tongues as the Spirit gave them utterance, but this power was not strictly for that purpose but that they would be endowed with power, authority, and boldness to continue the work of Jesus on this earth. Jesus had informed them that he was to go away but that he would not leave them without some help. He would send them the Holy Spirit. On the day of Pentecost this promise was fulfilled and Peter stood up with holy boldness to let the naysayers know that "We are not drunk as you think of drunkenness – but this is the work of the Holy Spirit. God is at work in us and through us.

And it is with this understanding that there is a deliberateness to everything which Peter and John said and did. They looked intently at the lame man. They instructed him to look at them. They said that they possessed no silver or gold, but they did have that which they would freely give to him. Immediately Peter commanded the man to stand up and walk in the name of Jesus Christ, the Nazarene. Peter then seized the man by the right hand and raised him up. Peter gave the man a hand-up.

In the name of Jesus Christ of Nazareth, you and I who have tasted of the power of the Holy Spirit have the authority to tell the lame that they can walk and the blind that they can see. We may not have money but we have power – the power of the Word of God, the power of God's love, the power of the Holy Spirit that can break every chain. In the name of Jesus, use your power, share your power. Speak the Word so that lives will be transformed.

The man who had never walked before in his life stood up with a leap, and he didn't quit leaping. What a sight that must have been. Some men would probably have dealt with such a miracle with great dignity and composure. Here was a man who had, for his whole life, been a spectacle. He earned his living by making a spectacle of himself, by drawing men's attention to his pitiable state. Now this man would surely care little that everyone was staring at him. He threw all caution to the wind, for he leaped about, clinging to Peter and John, praising God. It was a sight no one in the vicinity could have avoided. No wonder a crowd was attracted.

God had marvelously prepared this scene. The healed man had spent his life (or a good deal of it, it would seem) around the temple, begging. Everyone knew him – they couldn't have avoided him. The man, and his condition, were well known by all who frequented the temple (cf. 4:16, 21). And the fact that he had been crippled from his mother's womb was more than ample evidence that he was hopelessly disabled, and thus the miracle was a spectacular one. The people who witnessed this were understandably filled with wonder and amazement.

This man had asked for a hand-out but he got a hand-up. He would have been satisfied with just reaching his quota of alms for the day to return at another time as he had so often done to resume his life's work of begging. But on this day when he asked for a hand-out, but he got a hand-up. There is a saying that "if you give a man a fish he will eat for today, but if you teach the man to fish he will eat for a lifetime." If you give him a hand-out he will remain dependent, but if you teach him and provide him with the necessary skills he will be able to build upon it and provide for himself.

You and I have the power to speak the Word. It is a word that gives people a hand-up. For those who feel that they are unlovable, God's word comes to let them know that "For God so loved [you] the world, that God gave his only begotten son, that whosoever believeth in him should not perish but have everlasting life." For those who are paralyzed by feeling guilt and shame, speak the word, "For if we confess our sins, God is just to forgive us of our sins and to cleanse us from all unrighteousness."

We may not have money, but we have power – the power of the Word of God, the power of the Love of God, the power of God's healing and transformative power. Instead of giving people a hand-out that ignores their true situation, give them a hand-up and tell them that God loves them. Tell them that God has something better for their life. Tell them that they can make it. Tell them that there is a better way than the way that they are going.

And then be ready to roll up your sleeves and demonstrate through your investment of time that God is indeed concerned about them. Be prepared to give them a hand-up through mentoring and tutoring. Provide them with guidance. If you have the skill, teach them to improve their reading or help them to construct their résumé in search of a job. Help them prepare for a job interview. Teach them how to be respectful towards others, especially towards women. When they ask for a hand out, give them a hand-up.

Let me close with Jesus' example of giving us a hand-up. It is found in an old song: "I was sinking deep in sin, far from the peaceful shore, very deeply stained within, sinking to rise no more; but the Master of the sea heard my despairing cry, from the waters lifted me—now safe am I. Love lifted even me, Love lifted even me, when nothing else could help, Love lifted me; Love lifted me."[1]

God's love will give you a hand-up in this life. God's love will lift you higher above your faults, guilt, and shame. God's love is the greatest hand-up. If you're looking for a hand-out, I'm here to tell you that God is here to give you a hand-up to encourage you in this life. You're asking for a hand-out, but God is here to give you a hand-up. Give God your right hand and experience his awesome power, for God is here to give you a hand-up.

### Note

1. James Rowe, "Love Lifted Me" in Yes, Lord: Church of God in Christ Hymnal (Memphis, TN: Church of God in Christ Publishing Board, 1982), #425.

Refocus...

***Refocus*** is to adjust again to make an image clear; to cause (something, such as attention) to be directed at something different (Merriam-Webster online dictionary). The soul of Black men must be redeployed for the advancement of God's kingdom. There needs to be a global agenda that seeks to change the essence of a man's self-awareness of his relationship to the plans of God for his life and his role as a priest of his family and immediate community. Too many of our strong and powerful men have lost sight of their purpose and potential. This book of sermons seeks to help us transfer our personal and self-centered aspirations by shifting our focus from our problems unto/toward the power and promises of God.

When something is out of focus it is distorted. What you see is not necessarily what is. Only when you can see clearly, can you determine what truly exists. This is not only true in photography, but in life as well. What picture do you see for your life? You may need to *Refocus* on the big picture. As you frame this picture realize that you must think in a manner that is different from the past. Think about the end of your life. What would you have wanted to accomplish? What legacy will you leave to the world? These questions will cause you to change direction. To think, to plan, and to determine what needs to be done going forward. Remember a *Refocus* takes a "renewing of your mind" (Romans 12:2). It is clear that to *Refocus* means to make a shift in thinking, feelings, and taking actions that will cause a life to be a model for family (biological, spiritual, and extended). One must concentrate on what is good, and begin to see a new you.

We have some biblical guidance from Ecclesiastes 6:12, *"For who knoweth what is good for man in this life, all the days of his vain life which he spendeth as a shadow? For who can tell a man what shall be after him under the sun?"* and from Micah 6:8, *"He hath shewed thee, O man, what is good; and what doth the LORD require of thee, but to do justly, and to love mercy, and to walk humbly with thy God?"*

**REFOCUS**! Adjust your thinking. Find a trusted friend and accountability partner—one who is already exhibiting the strength, character, capabilities that you would like to have. Begin to develop a clear direction in which you should be headed and be tenacious in getting to your destiny. This is entirely possible when you *Refocus*!

After God restores a man, inevitably there should be a change in a man's focus. There should be a shift in thought, attitude, direction and perspective on God's purpose for his life. How do we accomplish this? We re-direct and refocus on God by seeking Him with all of our hearts, minds, bodies and soul. In doing this, God will meet our needs, and because of our obedience to Him, He will give us the desires of our hearts. Do we have our priorities established according to God's Word? If we put God first in all that we do, God will bless our lives and our efforts.

Matthew writes,

*"But seek ye first the kingdom of God, and his righteousness; and all these things shall be added unto you. Take therefore no thought for the morrow; for the morrow shall take thought for the things of itself. Sufficient unto the day is the evil thereof"* (Matthew 6:33-34).

Man must re-focus and place his faith and trust in God. In troubling times, all too often, man's focus has placed God secondary in his life; however, we are instructed to refocus on the Word of God so our focus will be on pleasing the Father. Our attention, efforts and service must be focused back on God. In pleasing God, we will find a state of peace that is immeasurable. We are instructed to be transformed by the renewing of our minds. When we intentionally re-direct our focus to God, and on what God wants us to do, we realize that we cannot be conformed to things that are oppositional to God's plan. God wants our body, mind, heart and soul committed and dedicated to His service. Apostle Paul instructs us when he writes,

*"I beseech you therefore, brethren, by the mercies of God, that we present your bodies a living sacrifice, holy, acceptable unto god, which is your reasonable service. And be not conformed to this world; but be ye transformed by the renewing of your mind, that ye may prove what is that good and acceptable, and perfect, will of God"* (Romans 12:1-2).

It is reasonable that we refocus on God, and put in perspective the plan of God for our life. Refocusing on the Word and will of God brings inner peace of our souls. Paul writes in Philippians,

*"And the peace of God, which passeth all understanding shall keep your hearts and minds through Christ Jesus"* (Philippians 4:7).

# On Becoming A Soul Man

*Kip Banks*

Genesis 2:7


*Cultural* critic and New York Village Voice writer Nelson George has said that we are now living in the Post-Soul era. This term "post-soul" is intended to describe the present cultural position of Blacks in America. By "post-soul," we mean that no longer is Black America based within a "soul tradition" that is implicitly and explicitly tied to the black religious tradition defined by the institution known as the black church.

You see, there was a time when everything in the black community came from the church. Our first educators and educational institutions like Morehouse College and Howard University came out of the church. The first financial institutions, business and philanthropic organizations came out of the church. Our political leaders came out of the church. Hirriam Revels, the first black U.S. Senator, came of the church. Adam Clayton Powell Jr. and Dr. Martin Luther King Jr. came out of the church. Andrew Young came out of the church. Even our music came out of the church. Sam Cooke came out of the church, Aretha Franklin came out of the church. Dionne Warwick came out of the church. Earth, Wind and Fire came out of the church. Stevie Wonder came out of the church. And this is why the music that they sang was known as "soul music"; it was soul music because it spoke to your soul!

Let me give you a couple examples. In the old days, the OJays would sing: "For the love of money people will steal from their mother. For the love of money people will rob their own brother." That's soul, that's biblical; the Bible says the love of money is the root of all evil. Or this one by Marvin Gaye: "Mother, mother, there's too many of you crying. Brother, brother, there's far too many of you dying. You know we've got to find a way, to bring some lovin' here today." That was soul music; it ministered to your soul! You could listen to it and there was a message in the music, a message that left you better off. The music came from the religious tradition of the church.

And at the time, these soul songs were the most popular songs on the billboard charts, but now the dominant form of music is not soul music but hip-hop music. And instead of being warned about the dangers of loving money and told about the danger of war, many of the primary messages of hip-hop are crass materialism, self gratification, narcissism, violence, and lust. We are in a "post-soul" era, and it ought to disturb you. This hip-hop gangsta culture is becoming the most dominant form of culture for young African American men, and it is assisting in the destroying our young people. And it's not just the dominant culture form for black people but also for white people, and it's influencing culture around the world. Something we need to understand is that African American culture influences white culture, because what others see us doing is what they consider to be cool. Listen to what journalist Patricia Hersch described as going on in white suburbia in her book *A Tribe Apart: A Journey into the Heart of American Adolescence*:

> It's hip-hop in suburbia, the culture of rap. Everywhere students wear baseball caps turned backwards or pulled down over their eyes, oversize T-shirts, ridiculously baggy jeans or shorts with dropped crotches that hang to mid-shin, and waists that sag to reveal the tops of brightly colored boxers.... "do rags," bandannas tied on the head, a style copied from street gangs.[1]

Hersch goes on to say that "black rage" is in style for white middle class kids because they find black inner-city street style to be the authentic way to be. One white kid living in Reston, Virginia, said we are living in the gangsta- generation. The hip gangta culture has overtaken our nation and even the world and we are living in a "Post-Soul" era.

But there's good news on the horizon, and that is that soul is poised to make a comeback, and this is because a brother who is a product of the soul era, a product of the black church, former Senator Barack Obama, was elected to the Presidency of the United States. He is setting the cultural standard, and now all of a sudden being a black man, being a soul brother, is in vogue. It's in style to be a black man; so much so, the November GQ has an article about white guys looking to rent black friends, because it's now in fashion again to be a soul man.

But what does it mean to be a soul brother? Does it mean that you know the latest hand shake, that you know how to give dap or the latest chest bump...or does it mean that you're able to say, the old school saying that we did back in the day "give me five, on the black hand side, in the hole...

you got soul!" Try that with your neighbor.... And you know we know how to do all kinds of ….but is that what makes you a soul brother?

To be a soul man is to not follow the example depicted in the popular media. In the movie *Soul Men*, the actors are supposedly critical of the hip-hop culture, but if you watch this very profane movie, the old stereotype plays out that a soul brother uses profanity and a soul brother drives a Cadillac, that a soul brother is a ladies man – in essence a pimp, that a soul man ignores his children, and that a soul man is into bullets, booze, blunts, and bars. These are the things that are killing our people. It's not only the bullets, it's also the bars that are killing our people. It's the mandatory minimum sentencing that is  jeopardizing the future of too many of our young men. It's the blunts and the booze. Too many are wasting away on alcohol and drugs; however, God has got a word for His people! He tells us what it means to be a soul man.

> *Then God said, "Let us make man in our image, in our likeness, and let them rule over the fish of the sea and the birds of the air, over the livestock, over all the earth, and over all the creatures that move along the ground."*
>
> *So God created man in his own image, in the image of God he created him; male and female he created them.*
>
> *God blessed them and said to them, "Be fruitful and increase in number; fill the earth and subdue it. Rule over the fish of the sea and the birds of the air and over every living creature that moves on the ground."* (Genesis 1:26-28)

### Reflect the Image of Jesus

Then God said, "Let us make man in our image, in our likeness." To be a soul man is to reflect the image of Jesus. God is a spirit and they that worship him must worship him in spirit and in truth. A soul brother has the love of Jesus, a soul brother has the joy of Jesus, a soul brother has the peace of Jesus, a soul brother has the patience of Jesus, a soul brother has the kindness of Jesus, a soul brother has the mind of Jesus, a soul brother walks like Jesus, a soul brother talks like Jesus, a soul brother works like Jesus, a soul brother serves like Jesus, a soul brother is meek like Jesus, a soul brother is holy like Jesus. Do you want to be like Jesus?

### Rule with the Authority of Christ

Then God said, "Let us make man in our image, in our likeness, and let them rule over the fish of the sea and the birds of the air, over the livestock, over all the earth, and over all the creatures that move along the ground." To be a soul man is to understand that Jesus has all authority. In the great commission he said all authority has been given to me, go therefore and make disciples of all nations. God has authority, and he expects us to go as his ambassadors. A soul brother rules with the authority of Christ. The problem is that we are rulers but we have abdicated our throne, and we are ruling in the wrong place. Dr. Jawanza Kunjufu, author of *Adam! Where Are You? Why Most Black Men Don't Come to Church*, has said that we are too often trying to rule in the area of sports, we are more concerned with football than faith, more concerned with the baseball than belief, more concerned with hoops than the holy Ghost, more concerned about Tiger Woods and the Masters than the Master, more concerned about Sunday sleep than salvation, more concerned about washing our cars than coming to church. But God expects us to rule with the compassion of Christ in our homes and on our jobs, and God expects us to rule with the compassion of Christ in the church. God has created us to rule. The problem is that we have abdicated our responsibility, thrown it aside, instead deciding to reign in sports and in the cars that we drive.

God has created us to be in leadership, not just in our homes, not just on our jobs, but in the church as well! As men, there's some work for us to do. Some young man who needs a father figure. We have to understand that for Christians there is never any unemployment. God wants us to be on the battlefield. I am on the battlefield for my Lord, I am on the battlefield for my Lord, and I promised him that I would serve him till I die. I am on the battlefield.

### Live in the Blessing of God

"God created man in his own image, in the image of God he created him; male and female he created them. God blessed them and said to them, 'Be fruitful and increase in number; fill the earth and subdue it.'" A soul man is one who has sex within the blessing of God. Have sex with the blessing of God. God blessed them, and said be fruitful and multiply. God blessed them. That signifies that the act of marriage is an act of getting God's blessing. God created sex, and sex is a good thing, but it is to be done in the context of marriage, with the blessing of God.

Every man has a battle against sexual temptation. If you say you don't have a battle then you lost it already, especially in this culture. If we get this under control we can be soul men. Any husband can make himself irresistible to his wife by learning to meet her seven basic marital needs:

- She needs for you to be a spiritual leader – a man of courage, conviction, commitment, compassion, and character; a man who takes the initiative in cultivating a spiritual environment for the family; a man who becomes a capable and competent student of God's Word and lives out before all a life founded on the Word of God; a man who leads his wife in becoming a woman of God and who takes the lead in training his children in the things of the Lord (Psalm 1, Ephesians 5:23-27).

- She needs personal affirmation/appreciation. Praise her attributes and qualities. Extol her virtues as a wife and as a mother. Commend her in the presence of others.

- She needs romance. Shower her with a steadfast flow of words, cards, flowers, and gifts, and not just on your anniversary.

- She needs intimate conversation. Talk with her heart to heart. Listen to her thoughts with interest and care.

- She needs honesty and openness.

- She needs protection and provision.

- She needs family commitment. Single men, understand that Paul says in 1 Corinthians that it's a good thing to be single, but understand that sex outside of marriage is sin, and if you are able to contain yourself, God can use you, but if you can't then you need to pray that God will send you the women whom he wants you to be with! Today more than 70% of our children, more than 2 of 3, are born out of wedlock. There are too many young men with no father in their lives. God is calling you to pay your child support. God is calling you to be a father figure to some young man, or some young woman.

What does it mean to be a soul man? It means that you reflect the image of Christ, it means that you rule with his authority, and it means that you have sex within the context of the blessings of God and that you are working to bring up children in the fear and admonition of the Lord. And one more thing. The Bible tells us: "And the LORD God formed man of the dust of the ground, and breathed into his nostrils the breath of life; and man became a living soul." To be a soul man you need to have the breath of God on the inside of you. You need to be filled with the Holy Ghost. If you receive Jesus as the Lord and savior of our life, repent of your sins, and place your trust in his death, burial, and resurrection, then you will be saved and receive the Holy Ghost. If you want to be a soul man, let the Holy Spirit rule.

*Breathe on me, Breath of God,*
*fill me with life anew,*
*that I may love what Thou dost love,*
*and do what Thou wouldst do.*

*Breathe on me, Breath of God,*
*until my heart is pure,*
*until with Thee I will one will,*
*to do and to endure.*

*Breathe on me, Breath of God,*
*till I am wholly Thine,*
*till all this earthly part of me*
*glows with Thy fire divine.*

*Breathe on me, Breath of God,*
*so shall I never die,*
*but live with Thee the perfect life*
*of Thine eternity.*[2]

Notes

1.  Patricia Hersch, A Tribe Apart: A Journey into the Heart of American Adolescence (New York: Ballantine Books, 1999), 82.

2.  Edwin Hatch, "Breathe on Me, Breath of God."

# Man: Created for Kingship!

*Hezekiah Walker*

1 Samuel 16

*As we view* God's divine plan for man it's very important that we recognize the importance of why man was created. I believe that God's divine plan for man is to proclaim the Gospel of the Kingdom of Jesus the Christ throughout the world and to live independently from the systems of this world. I also believe that we were created to maximize our fullest potential in life so that we may become empowered to subdue and to take authority and have dominion over this earth as a king with a Kingdom.

After the creation of man, man was such a thought on God's mind until Satan himself tried to distort God's mind about man through man. In this season of life your creation and kingship should be the center of your thoughts, because your divine positioning of your very existence is ever before Satan. He is the lost worshiper and he contends against you for his position back. Your fight has never been over what you have—your family, wife, children, money, cars, etc.; it has always been about your position and your kingship on earth. I told somebody the other day that Satan must want my place in the kingdom very bad because he refuses to let up off me. I then realized that his revenge is even greater than me; it's about Man. Who is man that thou are mindful of him? (Psalm 8:3-4).

The Bible says in the book of Job (14:1), *"Man born of a woman is but a few days and full of trouble."* This trouble is birthed out of the anger of Satan to refocus our attention from the position to the problem. But I refuse to allow Satan to redirect my thoughts and diminish my kingship as a man. As a man you must always keep in mind that you were created to have dominion and rulership. I refuse to be that man who sits around and wastes time dealing with trouble and problems when I've been crafted by God and empowered by the Holy Spirit to be and become a problem solver. Man was not created by God to waste or abuse time but to make time work in his favor. When man comes to the realization that God in creation fortified him to deal with trouble then his everyday problems will become his stepping stone to greatness.

In the text we see David as a shepherd boy attending to the sheep remaining in the place that was appointed to him. Meanwhile all of his brothers were out trying to find their place. Whenever man is out of place, he will always be in constant search for place. That's why it's very important as a man to stay in place with God. The children of Israel wandered in the wilderness for 40 years because they were out of place. How many times have all of us been out of place? And because of it we missed so many great opportunities and hundreds of open doors.

Staying in your place will grant you favor that's not privy to most. Sometimes staying in place will dictate that you are the least of everyone when in fact you are the head of everyone. Following God and staying in your place and waiting for your next assignment has become so obsolete that most deem it as "old school" or deep , but I would rather wait on God than lean to my own understanding. As the prophet waited to anoint one of Jesse's sons to be king, Jesse chooses his most likely sons to pass by the prophet and none of them was the one selected by God.

What I have come to realize is that God always chooses the unlikely. It's normally never the one that everyone wants or likes but it's always the least among them all. David wasn't like any of his brothers. He didn't look like them, he wasn't as tall as them, but he was the chosen one. Even Jesse doubted his own son's kingship, but kingship is not decided by man's opinion but by God's creation. David's kingship was upon him before the prophet anointed him.

While David was tending the sheep as a shepherd boy he was yet a king. As a man your status is not because of the position you have outwardly but the position you have inwardly. It is amazing to consider the mindset of God. God the creator of heaven and earth is so great and vast in comparison to mankind. If you were to look into God's mind, what would we behold? I would like to believe that you would see a mere reflection of mankind operating at its God-intended capacity.

Satan has always opposed man's positioning in the eye and heart of God. Remember God's view of David was that he was a man after God's heart and so is man. Man is divinely complex and supernaturally empowered. We, as man, have the power to decree, to prosecute, and to vindicate whatever shall be in the earth. Whatever God creates has purpose and within each creation purpose is extended; it's what I call unlimited limitations. This is man's ability to operate within the realm that God has provided us rulership.

We see this in creation, when God creates man in His image and after His likeness. We are the visible representation and the governmental essence of God on the earth. With this in mind we must be mindful that we do not neglect God or his directives. Although we have been made kings through creation God still is King of kings. Men were not made for the world but rather the world was made for man. We are His subordinates that he relies on us to help execute His will.

We are God's fingerprint within the earth. Man is proof that God existed and exists. We must be careful to rule well and to perpetuate kingship. Man's truest potential is always taken for granted. Often we are mentally robbed of our true kingship by society and its stereotypes and statistics. One of Jesse's sons tailored the form of what a king should be. There's always a "Samuel" whom God will put in man's life to ratify his kingship.

Samuel is the person who carries God's order of not looking at the common attributes of people's expectations. Samuel speaks to purpose and potential, not to opinions and impressions. Man must be confident in what God has put in his care. When we lose our focus we put in place the potential for us lose our kingdom. If David would have allowed the neglect of his father and brothers to affect him, he would have neglected the significance of his assignment to tend to the sheep. Had he not been in place when Samuel sent for him he would have missed his window of opportunity.

There's a part of man that struggles with the fact that he was born to rule. The devil plays on man's emotions to make us believe that we are not who God created us to be. When Satan wins the battle, we lose out on chief purpose as sons of God. The purpose is our kingship. "The LORD does not see as mortals see; they look on the outward appearance, but the LORD looks on the heart" (1 Samuel 16:7). To God be the Glory.

# A Call to Arms

*Harold Hudson*

Jude 1:7

***Since*** the author of this epistle was the brother of James, this would make him the half brother of our Lord Jesus Christ. Jesus' brothers in the flesh did not believe in Him while He was ministering here on earth. But after the Resurrection, James was converted, and we have every reason to believe that Jude was also saved at that time. Acts 1:14 informs us that "His brethren" were part of the praying group that was awaiting the Holy Spirit, and 1 Corinthians 9:5 states that "the brethren of the Lord" were known in the early church.

Why did Jude write this letter? Jude wrote this letter to warn his readers that the apostates were already on the scene! Peter had prophesied that they would come when he wrote 2 Peter 2:1-3 and 3:3, and his prophecy had been fulfilled. So apparently Jude wrote to the same believers who had received Peter's letters, intending to stir them up and remind them to take Peter's warnings to heart. He wrote to "exhort" them, to encourage them, and to strengthen them. In the Greek language, the word "exhort" was used to describe a general giving orders to the army, so the atmosphere and tone of this letter is "military" talk and style. Jude had started to write a quiet devotional letter about salvation, but the Spirit led him to put down his harp, The Spirit led him to stop being nice, the Spirit led him to quit being goody two shoes, and the Spirit led him to sound the trumpet!

The Epistle of Jude is a call to arms. The Captain of the army is Jesus Christ, and the soldiers He commands are people who share a "common salvation" through faith in Him. Jude called them saints in verse 3, which simply means "set-apart ones." He addressed them as sanctified, which, again, means "set apart." Paul tells us in Romans 9:16 that one thing that we can all be certain about is that salvation begins in the heart of God and not in the will of man. The mysteries of God's sovereign electing grace are beyond us in this life and will never be understood until we enter His glorious presence in eternity. For that reason, we are wise not to make them the basis for arguments and divisions.

Deuteronomy 29:29 tells us, "The secret things belong unto the Lord our God" and not to us. Second Thessalonians 2:13-14 makes it clear that the same God who chose us also set us apart by the Spirit and then called us by the Gospel to trust in Jesus Christ. God's choosing and God's calling go together, for the God who ordains our salvation also ordains the *means to the end*.

We did not understand how God's Spirit was working in our lives prior to our conversion, but He was working just the same to "set us apart" for Jesus Christ. Not only are God's saints set apart, but they are also *preserved*. This means "carefully watched and guarded." The believer is secure in Jesus Christ. This same word is used in Jude 6 and 13 and also in Jude 21, "keep yourselves." God is preserving the fallen angels and the apostates for judgment, but He is preserving His own children for glory. Meanwhile, He is able to preserve us in our daily walk and keep us from stumbling. Because they are set apart and preserved, God's soldiers are the recipients of God's choicest blessings: mercy, peace, and love. Like the Apostle Peter, Jude wanted these special blessings to be *multiplied* in their lives (1 Peter 1:2; 2 Peter 1:2). God in His mercy does not give us what we deserve. Instead, He gave our punishment to His own Son on the cross. "Surely He hath borne our griefs, and carried our sorrows.... But He was wounded for our transgressions, He was bruised for our iniquities" (Isaiah 53:4-5).

Because of Christ's work on the cross, believers enjoy peace. The unsaved person is at war with God and cannot please Him (Romans 8:7-8); but when he trusts the Lord, the war ends and he receives God's peace (Romans 5:1). He also experiences God's love (Romans 5:5). The Cross is God's demonstration of love (Romans 5:8), but His love is not experienced within us until His Spirit comes into the believing heart. As the believer grows in his spiritual life, he enters into a deeper relationship of love (John 14:21-24).

Certainly those who know Christ as their Savior enjoy a unique position. They are called *by* God to be set apart *for* God that they might enjoy love *with* God. While their fellowship with the Father might change from day to day, their relationship as children cannot change. They are "preserved in Jesus Christ." Because Jude would write a great deal in this letter about sin and judgment, he was careful at the very outset to define the special place that believers have in the heart and plan of God. The apostates would sin, fall, and suffer condemnation; but the true believers would be kept safe in Jesus Christ for all eternity.

It bears repeating that an apostate is not a true believer and he has abandoned his salvation. He is a person who has professed to accept the truth and trust the Savior, and then turns from "the faith which was once delivered unto the saints" (Jude 3). Jude would not contradict what Peter wrote, and Peter made it clear that the apostates were not God's sheep, but were instead pigs and dogs (2 Peter 2:21-22). The sow had been cleaned on the outside, and the dog on the inside, but neither had been given that new nature which is characteristic of God's true children.

Jude addresses God's "spiritual army." If you have trusted Jesus Christ, you are in this army. God is not looking for volunteers; He has already enlisted you! The question is not, "Shall I become a soldier?" Rather, it is, "Will I be a loyal soldier?" Isaac Watts once preached a sermon on 1 Corinthians 16:13: "Watch ye, stand fast in the faith, quit you [act] like men, be strong." When he published the sermon, he added a poem to it; we sing it today as one of our spiritual songs:

> *Am I a soldier of the Cross,*
> *A follower of the Lamb?*
> *And shall I fear to own His cause*
> *Or blush to speak His name?*
>
> *Must I be carried to the skies*
> *On flow'ry beds of ease?*
> *While others fought to win the prize*
> *And sailed through bloody seas?[1]*

Jude set out to write an encouraging letter about "the common salvation." The name Jude (Judah) means "praise," and he was anxious to praise God and rejoice in the salvation God gives in Jesus Christ. But the Spirit of God changed his mind and led Jude to write about the battle against the forces of evil in the world. Why did the Spirit change Jude's mind? His mind was changed because it was "needful" for the church. I must confess this morning that I sympathize with Jude. In my own ministry, I would much rather encourage the saints than declare war on the apostates. But when the enemy is in the field, the watchmen dare not go to sleep. The Christian life is a battleground, not a playground.

Jude wasted no time in identifying the enemy:

- Jude said they were ungodly. This is one of Jude's favorite words. While these men *claimed* to belong to God, they were, in fact, ungodly in their thinking and their living. They might have "a form of godliness," but they lacked the *force* of godliness that lives in the true Christian.

- Jude said they were deceitful. They "crept in unawares." The Greek word means "to slip in secretly, to steal in undercover." Sometimes Satan's undercover agents are *"brought in* secretly" by those already on the inside, Paul says in Galatians 2:4, but these men came in on their own. Peter had warned that these men were coming, and now they had arrived on the scene. How could false brethren get into true assemblies of the saints? *The soldiers had gone to sleep at the post!* The spiritual leaders in the churches had grown complacent and careless. This explains why Jude had to "blow the trumpet" to wake them up. Our Lord and His Apostles all warned that false teachers would arise, yet the churches did not heed the warnings. Sad to say, some churches are not heeding the warnings today.

- Jude said they were enemies of God's grace. They entered the church to attempt to change the doctrine and "turn the grace of our God into *lasciviousness"* (Jude 4). The word lasciviousness simply means "wantonness, absence of moral restraint, indecency." A person who is lascivious thinks *only* of satisfying his lusts, and whatever he touches is stained by his base appetites. Lasciviousness is one of the works of the flesh that proceeds from the evil heart of men and women. Peter had already warned these people that the apostates would argue, "You have been saved by grace, so you are free to live as you please!" They promised the people freedom, but it was the kind of freedom that led to terrible bondage. The apostates, like the cultists today, use the Word of God to promote and defend their false doctrines. They seduce young, immature Christians who have not yet been grounded in the Scriptures. Every soldier of the Cross needs to go through "basic training" in a local church so that he or she knows how to use the weapons of spiritual warfare.

- Jude said they denied God's truth. Jude was not writing about two different persons when he wrote "the only Lord God, and our Lord Jesus Christ," for the Greek construction demands that these two names refer to one Person. In other words, Jude was affirming strongly the deity of Jesus Christ. Jude was saying that Jesus Christ is God! But the apostates would deny this. They would agree that Jesus Christ was a good man and a great teacher, but not that He was the eternal God come in human flesh. The first test of any religious teacher, as we have seen, is, "What do you think of Jesus Christ? Is He God come in the flesh?" Anyone who denies this cardinal doctrine is a false teacher *no matter how correct he or she may be in other matters.* If they deny the deity of Christ, then something will always be missing in whatever they affirm.

- Jude said that they were ordained to judgment. Jude did not write that these men were ordained to become apostates, as though God were responsible for their sin. They became apostates because they willfully turned away from the truth. But God did ordain that such people would be judged and condemned. The Old Testament prophets denounced the false prophets of their day, and both Jesus Christ and His Apostles pronounced judgment on them. Why should these men be judged by God? To begin with, they had denied His Son! That is reason enough for their condemnation! But they had also defiled God's people by teaching them that God's grace permitted them to practice sin. Furthermore, they derided the doctrine of Christ's coming. They would say, "Where is the promise of His coming?" They mocked the very promise of Christ's coming and the judgment He would bring against the ungodly. Of course, they did all these things under the disguise of religion, and this made their sin even greater. They deceived innocent people, so that they might take their money and enjoy it in godless living. Jesus compared them to wolves in sheep's clothing in Matthew 7:15.

How should the church respond to the presence of this insidious enemy? Jude says the church should respond by earnestly contending for the faith. "The faith" refers to that body of doctrine that was given by God through the Apostles to the church. This is a call to arms that Jesus gave on Calvary. When He was carrying His cross, that was a call to arms. When He was hung up high, that was a call to arms. When they stuck Him in His side, that was a call to arms. When they buried Him in a tomb, that was a call to arms.

But when Sunday morning came, that was an answer to the call. His Father called Him, and He got up on Sunday morning. And we are called to arms, called to be a soldier of the cross.

> Are there no foes for me to face?
> *Must I not stem the flood?*
> *Is this vile world a friend to grace,*
> *To help me on to God?*
>
> *Sure I must fight if I would reign:*
> *Increase my courage, Lord;*
> *I'll bear the toil, endure the pain,*
> *Supported by Thy word.*[2]

Notes

1.   Isaac Watts, "Am I a Soldier of the Cross," verses 1 and 2.

2.   Ibid., verses 3 and 4.

# I'm Back and I'm Proud

*Melvin Cotton, Jr.*

Luke 15:11-32

*In the 1960s,* James Brown was known as the Godfather of Soul. He inspired people to celebrate the very thing they were being treated inhumane for – being Black. The song he inspired them with was *"I'm Black and I'm Proud."*

Bear with me as I take you on a journey back in time. In 1444, the first Europeans to visit a certain island were some Portuguese sailors. Not too long after that visit Europeans decided to settle on that island, which is named Goree. They drove out those who were inhabitants of the island. This island is located approximately 2 miles off the coast of Senegal, Africa. From 1536 to 1848, history tells us that this is the place where slaves were sold and shipped from Africa as if they were livestock. This is the place where somebody's great great great great great grandmother was chained up in the bottom of a ship to be sold so that she could reproduce and have children to be sold as slaves. This is an ugly truth. They wanted these women to "breed" some slaves. This is a moment in Black History.

Speaking in regards to history, African American history needs to be preached and taught all year long. Because of our history there is an urgency for the Gospel to be viewed through the eyes of African Americans. The historic site known as the "door of no return" was closed down in 1848. At that time the slave trade was abolished in Senegal. From the shores of Senegal to the various destinations along the European slave trade now known as the transatlantic slave trade, black people lost a lot of things. There was loss of life, love, peace, joy, and many other things.

One of the most important things lost was our identity. Whenever identity is lost, that creates a crisis of the soul. A crisis of soul is when the moral and emotional nature of a person is in need of serious attention. I sometimes get emotional and tear up when I give thought to this, but not today. Today I'm able to keep my composure, because I can see hope.

It is believed that the first slaves to reach the North American continent arrived in Jamestown, Virginia. In the historic towns of Colonial Williamsburg and Jamestown, workers at the exhibits tell visitors about the first English settlement; they tell about all the battles and things of that nature. If I had my way I would be telling people of all races about the selling of slaves right down the street from where we now purchase clothes and jewelry. Even though I am a lover of history, I don't talk much about Pangea, the gold rush, the Louisiana Purchase, the pilgrims or Christopher Columbus. How can somebody discover a place where people already lived, people whom they now call the Native Americans?

I'd rather talk about how black people got to America and what we've been through to get where we are and the challenges we still face trying to get where we want to go. Why is it that this particular portion of history is not often told? A lot of this history I've learned from elderly people throughout the years, because such history has been omitted in grade school. One of them was my grandfather John Alexander Plaskett, who was from an island called Saint Croix. I will never forget him saying to me, "Make something of yourself, because you have opportunities that I did not have growing up."

Along the way people of color have suffered the loss of many things. During the Civil Rights Movement, Americans of African descent experienced loss because of degradation, degeneration, depression, poverty, and racism. During these times there was not much to have hope in, but God.

For me not only was there my grandfather, but there were also some neighbors who were elderly and prayed for me on their porches as we split open butter beans and prepped other vegetables that we had gotten from their gardens. They prayed for me to stay on the right path. My mother, Myra A. Cotton, and father, Melvin Cotton, Sr., did all they could to keep me on the right path.

I said along the way we've lost some things, but I present this question to you: In your life, have you ever gotten lost?

The Gospel According to Luke is a very interesting piece of literature. Even though it is one of the three Synoptic Gospels, it is unique in its aim of the intended audience. In my own Afrocentric examination, the aim of the Gospel According to Luke is to reach the least, the lost, and the left out. That's not to say the other writers neglected to do so; however, Luke wrote directly to the Gentiles. Luke was a Gentile physician, so Luke wrote to his people, the Gentiles. His emphasis was based on proclaiming the humanity of Christ. Now, looking at the time in which the Gospel According to Luke was written, there was a lot of bigotry going on with the hate of the Jews towards the Gentiles. A Gentile was considered to be one who was not a child of God, had no hope for salvation, could not be used by God, and was despised by most Jews. So in the same regards as African Americans, the Gentiles were the least, the lost, and the left out. Even though Dr. Luke was a Gentile, not considered to be a child of God, looked at as not being capable of being used by God, despised by a lot of racist people, voted most likely not to succeed, he is the writer of the Gospel According to Luke.

Seeing that Luke could write a social Gospel intrigued me and made me realize all of us can write a Gospel. We have to keep in mind that the word "Gospel" means good news." The prepositional phrase "according to" gives contextual credibility. The Gospels were written about Jesus, who is the Good News. So if you are reading this, I believe you are a Gospel writer, because all of us can contextualize some credible Good News about Jesus. So Luke takes the time to tell his people who are considered the least, the lost, and the left out about a Man who could change their situation.

In the 15th chapter of the Gospel According to Luke, Jesus talks about three things that were lost: the lost coin, the lost sheep, and the lost son, whom we call the prodigal son. Many preachers have called this the lost-and-found chapter. My focus is on the son who had gotten lost. I have no problem admitting that I've been lost before. Have you ever been lost or lost your way?

Here in the text we see a young boy who was being raised up in a way that was considered to be the right way according to their culture. The Bible does not say there was a woman present and does not inform us of why she's not there. Maybe she was there and just wasn't mentioned or she could have passed away. But our focus is on the lost son and his relationship with his father.

There are times in our lives when in spite of our upbringing no matter how good it was from a biblical or parental view we sometimes get lost, and when such times occur all we have to do is go back home.

This text displays to us a child being raised under the rules and regulations of a parent who cares about the future of his child. I contextually argue the fact that this parent cared because he was following the law of the Jewish culture by leaving his children an inheritance. The inheritance according to Deuteronomy 21:17 was for the firstborn to get 2/3 of what the father owned and the second born to receive 1/3. They were not supposed to receive this until the father had died, but the younger son wanted his inheritance immediately. He desired his inheritance prematurely at a time of immaturity.

I applaud the father because he had something positive to leave his sons. As fathers, what are we leaving our children? In the text, the younger son was ready to go out and see what the world had to offer. I believe he felt he was missing something. Perhaps he had some restrictions. Maybe some young lady had been telling him how handsome he was. It is possible that some friends had been telling him that he was lame because he missed the party last weekend.

Excuse my real-life application, but I see my father and myself in the text. There was a period in my life when it was just my father and me. Maybe the younger son in the text got tired of a curfew, not being able to hang out with his boys, who meant him no good. Or this text could be about that Christian who is tired of waiting on his or her blessing and decides to take what God has already provided and live like the world. This child could be you. And in looking at the father in the text, what if you lost your child? There are many fathers living this reality as well as children living such a reality. We are living in a day when sons are screaming out for their fathers. The way in which sons are screaming for their fathers are by voices called trouble, drug dealing, drug abusing, degradation of women, dropping out of school, killing one another, incarceration, giving their mothers hell, etc.

The Bible informs us that this particular son went out and did some reckless living. He had worldly fun; he went out splurging his money/ inheritance that was set aside for a later time of maturity. He spent his money on whatever he desired.

This good boy has gone bad. He ends up broke and had too much pride to go home. He was in the world living beneath the status his father had established for him. Many of us as Christian fathers, men, and sons are living beneath the status that God the Father has provided for us.

When the famine came in the land, the Bible declares that the son began to be in need. He needed money, food, and a roof over his head. He became desperate. Have you ever been desperate? This text resonates with me so strongly and I can see myself in the text. He was so desperate that he took a job feeding pigs. Because of Jewish law, Jews had no dealings with pigs. So in other words he was so desperate he took whatever job he could find. It was a dead-end job and did not even pay him. He dwelled with the pigs and was expected to eat of their slop.

The Bible declares that he came to himself, which means he realized who he was and whose he was. He realized that he was a son and belonged to his father: "How many of my father's hired hands have bread and enough to spare, but here I am dying of hunger." I'm reminded of when David said, "I've never seen the righteous forsaken or his seed begging bread."

After the son remembered who he was and whose he was, he went home. The Bible tells us that when his father saw him afar off, his father recognized him, ran to him, and embraced him. His father could still recognize him beyond how he appeared. His father did not care what he looked like or smelled like.

As fathers, we need to run out and meet our sons where they are. We have to look beyond how many children they have fathered prematurely, look beyond the trouble they may have gotten into, look beyond the drug or alcohol abuse, and we must embrace our sons. A father should be gracious in understanding that we all make mistakes.

Even though his father embraced him, the son still had to repent, so he said, "Father, I have sinned and I am no longer worthy to be called your son." Look at this act of humility. As men we are famous for holding grudges. Brothers, we have to let some things go! Reflecting back on the text, after the young man apologizes and repents , his father showed him an act of redemption with a robe. As fathers we need to cover our sons and have their backs!

In the text at verse 29, the older son said to his father, "Listen, all these years I have been working like a slave for you and I have never disobeyed you, yet you have never given me a young goat so that I might celebrate with my friends. But when this son of yours came back, who has wasted your property with prostitutes (in other words the world), you killed the fatted calf for him." But the father replied, "Son, you are always with me, and all that is mine is yours. We had to celebrate and rejoice, because this brother of yours was spiritually dead and has come back to life. This brother of yours was lost and has now been found."

Brothers, I was once spiritually dead but now I am alive. I don't know about you, but I was lost, but one day I was found. At the age of 15 I had lost my way. I started hanging with the wrong crowd, hanging with the bootleggers, getting drunk, living the fast life, and disobeying my parents. But one day I realized who I was and whose I was. So I went home, and when I got home my father recognized me and embraced me. I was surprised that my father recognized me because I went through hell and I looked like hell.

I went back home with two babies. I went back home looking and smelling like where I had been. I went back home broke and hungry. I went back home in trouble. But my father looked beyond my fault and saw my need. He saw that I realized I needed my daddy, he saw that I realized I needed redemption. You don't know the hell I went through out there.

Many of us have loss and have gotten lost in this journey of life. We have to revive the soul of our manhood. The father in the text had a true soul of a father. The soul of a father that he exemplified is such a manner that God operates through him an example to us as men. God ordained us to proclaim the Good News of Jesus Christ to our families.

My Father covered me with a robe called the Blood. Not only did my family rejoice, but my Father, my Jesus, and the angels rejoiced. That's why I can say that I'm Back and I'm proud. They said that I was a waste, but look at me now. I've been covered, I'm Back and I'm proud. I know that God has brought you back from somewhere or something. So as you continue on this journey of life, don't be afraid to say it loud: "I'm Back and I'm proud."

# In the Midst of Our Pain

*Darryl D. Sims*

2 Corinthians 12:1-10

***The pain*** we experience in our lives can make us or break us. Our pain can bring us closer to God or make us desire to attempt to depart from God. Our pain can make us strong or it can make us weak. Our pain can drive us to love one another or it can drive us to hate one another. Our pain can prepare us for a spiritual battle or it can prepare us for a spiritual defeat. Pain can bring cohesion to a family or it can bring division to a family. Pain can make us rise to the occasion or it can make us run from the opposition. Pain can be the fertile soil for the production of our Christian development or it can be the quicksand in which our Christian development suffocates.

Pain can render you paralyzed. Pain has the potential to imprison your imagination, to hold captive your creativity, to defer your dreams, to manipulate your mind, to sideline you from your success. Within the church our pain can cause us to work harder for Christ or our pain can cause us to quit and simply shut down and do absolutely nothing except keep a pew warm and criticize everyone else who is at least trying to help with God's agenda.

Pain, heartache, broken spirits, disappointment, and discomfort are realities of life. However, solutions, resolutions, restoration, and reconciliation are realities as well. Hurting is a reality but so is healing. Fighting is a reality but so is forgiveness.

Arguing is a reality but so is accepting. Deceit is a reality but so is truth. Bitterness is a reality but so is sweetness. Crying is a reality but so is comfort. Falling is a reality but so is rising. Sin is a reality but so is salvation.

Facing a crisis is a reality, but so is the ever-abiding presence of God a reality! That is why how we view our God is so important. How we view our God will determine how we view our pain. How we view our God will determine how we view one another. How we view our God will determine how we view our trials and tribulations. If we view God as being able to do anything but fail then that should settle it. Either you believe that He can do all things but fail or you don't. We can't waver in our faith. We can't be lukewarm Christians. The Bible says that a double-minded man is unstable in all of his ways. This is why the Bible says let your yes be yes and your no be no. The worst decision that a Christian can make is no decision. Indecision is a tool of the adversary and is oftentimes more costly than a bad decision. We can't allow our pain to render us indecisive. We can't allow our pain to make us too afraid to continue in our dreams and pursuits. Whenever we place God into the equation of our pain, it will make all the difference. It doesn't matter where you are or what you're going through – God is a God who can help you make it over, and He is able to give you a spiritual makeover. When we attempt to look through the lenses of God's power and not just our pain, we are afforded the opportunity to see our potential and possibility. Then we will learn that discomfort and disappointments in our lives are nothing more than opportunities for God to display His awesomeness in our lives.

Pain and problems in our lives are nothing more than platforms for God to stand on His promises and perform miracles in our lives. The Bible declares that wherever the spirit of the Lord is—there is liberty. Trials and tribulations are nothing more than opportunities for God to test our trust in Him. God wants to know if you trust Him. Do you trust Him to do things that He said he would do and could do? Do you trust Him to be your friend when you feel friendless? Do you trust Him to be your bridge over troubled waters? Do you trust Him to deliver you from the devices of the devil? Do you trust Him to be your Bright and Morning Star? When things seem unbearable and life appears to be getting the best of you, do you trust Him to bring you through it? Do you rely on your finite wisdom or do you do what the Bible tells us to do in Proverbs 3:5-6: "Trust in the Lord with all thine heart; and lean not unto your own understanding. In all thy ways acknowledge Him, and He shall direct thy path."

Sometimes, especially when our stuff gets messy, our pain seems to outweigh His promises. When we allow ourselves to look more at our predicament than our Savior, we tend to fall down and fall away from Him. Just ask Peter, who asked Jesus to allow him to walk on the water. While his request was being granted, Peter took his eyes off of Jesus' presence and began to fall into the water, not because of the force and tempest of the waves, but because he took his eyes off the One who rules the wind and the water.

This is where so many of us fall short in our walk with Christ. All too often, we forget about God's wondrous working power and we start to focus more on the dangers around us, on what could go wrong, or what has gone wrong, and on the negative people in our lives. These are self-induced mind games that we play on ourselves. All too often, we allow ourselves to be our own worst enemy. All too often we validate our own demise, by allowing negative "what ifs" to override the positive "what ifs." We allow the pain in our life to play tricks on our mind.

How do we stay on track in spite of our pain? How do we help ourselves get control of our pain? What are the essential ingredients that will enable us to live a victorious life in the midst of our pain? How can a man stay on point in the midst of his pain? The text gives us some great insight on what we can find in the midst of our pain.

Paul shows us that the first thing we must do in the midst of our pain is own up to our pedigree. Said another way, acknowledge everything that you have gone through and accept it as preparation for making it the 'you' whom God desires you to be.

Paul took ownership of who he was, pain and all. Paul writes in chapter 11, starting around verse 22, that he's not ashamed of the color of his skin, for he says I am a Hebrew. He says I'm not ashamed of my roots in Africa, for he says I am an Israelite. He says I'm not ashamed of my ancestors, for I am a descendant of Abraham. He says I am not ashamed of my pedigree. I am a blue-collar worker; I sew tents. I am an ex-con and I have a record. I've been in prison more than once. I have been exposed to death more than most men. He goes on to say that he was beaten with whips by his Jewish brothers five times, beaten with rods three times, stoned once, and shipwrecked on three separate occasions. Paul isn't ashamed to express his defeats and his fears, for he says I have been in danger from the rivers, in danger from bandits, in danger from my own countrymen, in danger from the Gentiles, in danger in the city, in danger in the countryside, and in danger at sea. He says he has labored long hours and gone without sleep, he has known hunger and thirst on a first-name basis, and has been cold and naked on more occasions than he cares to remember.

I read you Paul's vitae to say to you OWN UP to all that you've gone through, for there is, in the midst of it all, a plan of God for your life. Don't suppress the painful memories of your past; allow God to convert your pain into your power. God may be trying to set you up to be a blessing to the world. But if you are stuck in your pain, instead of acknowledging it and moving past it, you will miss God's purpose for you. Sometimes the very thing that you view as too painful is the thing that God is going to use as a vehicle to bless you and others through you. Joseph's brothers threw him in a pit and sold him into slavery, but God used that experience to bless Joseph and the entire family of Israel. David was overlooked by his daddy, looked down on by his brothers, second-guessed by the prophet Samuel, and chased into a cave by

King Saul, but God used all of that to make him a better king. Why? Because David had enough sense to keep going back to God and owning up to all of who he was and owning up to all that had happened to him. He didn't dwell in or on any one bad experience. Instead he used his pain as a key card to gain entrance to God.

Peter denied the Lord three times and had his manhood stripped from him by a little girl who asked a simple question, "Do you know this Black barefoot preacher from Nazareth?" In the midst of Peter's pain and shame Peter could have gone home and said now everybody knows I'm a fake. But because he held on, the same Savior he denied restored him and gave him a leading role in expanding the Church of the Lord Jesus Christ. Peter went from Mr. Shackey Ground to Mr. Solid Ground. Christ said to him, "Upon this rock I will my Church."

We as Christians need to be reminded on this day that God is still a God of restoration, He's still a God of reconciliation, He's still a God of redemption. And what He has done for others He will do for you: He'll handcuff your negative experiences and convert them into positive feelings. He'll change your bitter memories into sweet refrains. He'll uproot your grief and show you how you can use it to give Him glory. You do remember Lazarus who was placed in a coffin. You do remember the three Hebrew boys who were thrown in a fiery furnace. You do remember Daniel who was thrown in the lions' den. But in the end all of their stories gave God glory. And that's what God wants from us today—some glory. Be who you are, own your entire life, and then let God use it to gain glory. God can get glory from your story.

Paul shows us that the second thing we must do in the midst of our pain is to acknowledge the power of prayer. Paul says in verse 8, "He had a thorn and three times he pleaded with the Lord to take it away from him." Our pain will force us to our knees. Our pain will force us to submit to God's will. Our pain will cause us to raise the question, "Is there a balm in Gilead?" Our pain will force us to look at ourselves and others differently. Our pain will cause us to pray, when it gets bad enough!

Why prayer? Because prayer still changes things! Prayer is that necessary conversation with God. Prayer is the opening of the windows to a person's heart. Prayer is the unlocking of the door to a person's mind. Prayer is that moment in your life when you don't care what anybody anywhere thinks of you. Prayer is when you are willing to go to God in the nakedness of your reality.

We all need to be willing to go before God in the nakedness of all our mess. Why? It is in our nakedness where we're more inclined to be truthful with God about all of our problems, predicaments, painful situations, and present sins. David went to God in prayer after his adulterous affair with Bathsheba. Daniel went to God in prayer after he was told that he couldn't worship his God. Deborah went to God in prayer to decide if she should go to war. Many of us refuse to take our mess to Jesus in prayer because our mess is extremely messy. We think if we don't talk about it then God won't know about it. He already knows your issues, struggles, and sinful pleasurable proclivities. He's waiting on you to own up to your messy and sinful situations. The Bible says that if we confess our sins, he is faithful and just to forgive us our sins and cleanse us from all unrighteousness. You need to confess that thing before you pray about that thing. Our pain and predicament will cause us to pray, and our prayer will prompt God to answer.

Have you ever asked someone for something and after you received it so much drama came with it that you wished you hadn't asked for it? Maybe you asked a young lady for her telephone number because she looked like Halle Berry, but after a few dates you saw that she was actually a very Scary Berry. For my sisters who like to read books written primarily for men, maybe you met a tall fine brother and thought you had a candidate for a sugar daddy, but after one date you discovered that he was looking for a sugar momma. Have you ever asked your boss for a promotion and received it, but hated the additional hours and responsibilities? Well, that's what many of us do with God—we go to the throne of grace asking for something, but we're not always ready for the response that God gives. God will always answer you in one of three ways: yes, no, or not yet. Sometimes we ask God for what we want, and God in His permissive will just grant that request. The problem is although God gave us what we asked for via His permissive will, it wasn't what He had designed and ordained for us in His perfect will! He gave it because He has a permissive will, but all too often, we miss out on the best stuff because we didn't want to wait patiently and seek God's perfect will.

My brothers, we need to stop asking God for what we want and start asking God for what He wants for us. Seek God's perfect will. That way, you know you will get all that God has for you. Paul is begging the Lord to remove a thorn from his life and God flat out says "NO!" Whenever you're seeking to be all that God will have you to be, there are some things you must simply stop asking God to remove from you and simply ask God to help navigate you through your situation, by way of your prayers. God truly is the authentic GPS system. He can navigate you to and through your pain.

The third thing we must do in the midst of our pain is to acknowledge the power of God's presence in the midst our pain. After Paul said that he prayed to the Lord three times asking God to remove this thorn from him. Paul says that the Lord not only told him that His grace is sufficient. Now, brothers, I don't know about you; but this wouldn't have been a sufficient answer for me. Honestly, I would have expected a little more from God.

Nevertheless, I wrote earlier, if you pray God will talk to you. God will, can, and often answers us in strange ways. He answered Elijah with a still small voice. He answered Moses with a thunderous voice. He showed up in Jacob's life in the form of an Angel. He communicated with Joseph via dreams. There aren't any limits on how God can answer you and/or reveal Himself in your situations. We know that God is omni-present, but we don't know how He's going to unwrap His presence. Every now and then God will show us His awesome power absent of His complete presence, because He wants us to understand that there is power included in just His essence.

Have you ever had a person walk past you and you could smell a sweet fragrance as they passed by? And long after they left the room you could still sense their presence by way of the aroma they left behind. That's how it is with God—once God passes through a situation, the complete manifestation of His presence is no longer required because His essence will always linger behind. And God's essence equals God's presence. He wants us to know this because there will be times when we will not be able to detect God or feel God in the midst of our lives, but that doesn't mean God isn't around. My mother would leave a note at home for us to read when she wasn't going to be home upon our arrival from school, and we knew what we had to do without her being present. Well, it's like that with God. God tells "Grace" what to do—when it's really not vital for God to be all up in our trials and tribulations or when God decides that some of our pain needs to be utilized, so our lives can be maximized. God simply instructs "Grace" to watch over us and sustain us. In other words, if God's grace is in it then the "it" that you're going through can't defeat you.

Translated another way, there is no pain on earth that heaven can't heal. There is no painful memory in your mind that heaven can't record over. There is no crooked turn in your life that God can't straighten out. There is no demon in your past that God can't defeat. There is no person in your life that God can't remove. But the best news of all is there is no sin that God can't forgive!

And if God can forgive your sins, then why can't you let go of the guilt? If God's grace covered it, then why do you keep bringing it back up? If God has cleansed you, then why are you allowing others to make you feel so dirty? If God has brought you out of it, then why are you allowing others to lead you back into it? If God has been your provider, then why are still looking for others to do for you what you can do for yourself?

My beloved brothers, stop expecting people to see life through your lenses. Just live your life where they can see the God in you and the power of God working through you! Let go of how you wish it could have been and simply deal with how things are, right now! Release it from your hands and He will deal with it for you. Give God a chance to be God. It is not by our goodness that we attain our victories; it is by His grace.

By His grace we can have life and have it more abundantly. By His grace we are clothed in our right mind and not buried in our grave. By His grace the Devil didn't take us out when he had the chance. By His grace we are able to raise our kids in the admonition of the Lord. By His grace we are able to love our women as the Queens they are. By His grace we can face our tomorrow. By His grace we can let go of our sorrow. By His grace we know victory is ours. By His grace we know Him as our friend. By His grace we have the right to call Him Lord of lords and King of kings.

> *Amazing Grace! how sweet the sound*
> *That saved a wretch like me!*
> *I once was lost but now I'm found,*
> *Was blind but now I see.*[1]

His grace saved me. His grace rescued me. His grace restored me. His grace carried me. His grace lifted me. His grace healed me. His grace leads me. His grace covers me. His grace holds me. His grace justifies me. His grace redeems me. By His grace we gained a Savior, who lived, died, and rose early on Sunday morning with all power in His Hands!

And it's because of His power that we have power. Power to walk right. Power to talk right. Power to live right. Power to give right. Power to love right. Power to be right.

Note

1.  John Newton, "Amazing Grace."

# Afterword

*Wallace Murray*

*In* John Steinbeck's story "Flight," the character of Pepe shows that, "A boy becomes a man when a man is needed." Too many of our boys are not required to become men. Let us examine and discover some of ways that we might aid our young men in becoming the men that they are going to need to be in order to provide and leave a more spiritual, civil, and prosperous society for the current and next generation of boys, young men, and leaders of the next great generation of young people.

Some have counted out the last generation as lost; however, therein lies an opportunity for change. Many see the brokenness of our young boys. Some of them feel hopeless in a time when technology is operating at a pace our grandparents could not have conceived as even been possible 50 years ago, and at the same time we have record violence in our neighborhoods, schools, and in the general concourses of everyday life. I submit that we have forgotten some of the basic tenets of the Bible that for generations great societies have used as a guide and in some cases the basis for their very existence.

It is not my desire to offend any with my next statement, however it is my deep intention to challenge you to change the tide of the product that this truth has produced in our children. So brace yourself for a fact that we must face. This is the truth that we must own: Most problems that our young people face today has as its genesis adults. Let me be more clear: Children do not provide drugs, adults do. Children do not provide guns, adults do. Children do not provide bad education, adults do. Children do not provide other children for sex slaves and trafficking, adults do. Children do not provide a horrific foster-care environment, adults do. Children do not produce, manufacture, distribute, and sell sexually driven and explicit music, movies and video games, adults do. Children do not provide broken homes, adults do.

In these cases it is my firm belief that adults need to fix what adults have broken. While it is terrible, we have the tools to fix this and it starts with the Bible. My Bible provided the necessary instructions and directives for the development of my manhood. Therefore, I was not to be negligent in sharing the same with my children. I leaned early in my years as a parent of three wonderful sons: I did not only have to teach and train my kids but I had the obligation to teach and train the ones whom they played with and the ones whom they were going to possibly emulate. I could not say that "I will only help my three sons and no more." I understood that my manhood was not attached exclusively to my possessions. The Bible raises an inquiry, "What good is for a man to gain the entire world and lose his soul? (Matthew 16:26)

Our young people have been left behind. We must own and identify who left them behind. Too often this is not addressed, so no one feels the accountability that would lead to action by the at-fault party. Our young were left behind by somebody. It is alright to admit failure, but it is not alright to abandon our young.

In some cases they were left behind by adults who refused to grow up and become good parents. They have been left behind by a system of education that does not always live up to its own creed. They are left to peril by a legal system that is supposed to protect but instead preys upon them at the time their discovery. The very nature of learning involves discovery and we can all attest that discovery will cause you to do some very stupid and immature things that we learn to later regret.

In guiding our boys to manhood, we must help them to become self-sufficient. I would like to examine the way the adult fox handles the detail of aiding his pup to take care of himself. The fox for the first portion of the pup's life cares for its every need—food, shelter, etc. The young does have to hunt for its food as the adult provides it for him. One day out to the blue the adult fox goes to get food for the pup, but when the adult returns it starts to become aggressive and he does not come with food as usual and he drives the pup away from the den that is the pup's home. All of the resources that the pup had come to expect his father to provide are halted immediately and without notice. This is an extreme way to require the pup to care for itself, but from it we can learn a lesson for our boys—that the requirement that our boys become men will not kill them; it will cause them to overcome and give a sense of accomplishment to the generation before them as well as giving them a full measure of what it means to be truly responsible and self-sufficient.

Jesus said, "I must be about my Father's business." He had a personal sense of destiny and desire that pushed him to want to be part of his community. We must play a supportive role in guiding our sons to manhood using the

Bible as the core of our belief system. We must have a standard for what we believe. We too often operate on feeling and not on the word of God. We have not taught our sons to take on the inheritance that the father has given them. Romans 4 tells us that we need faith to possess an inheritance.

John Adams believed in the following progression of study that he saw for his family and thus his community and society as a whole.

> The science of government it is my duty to study, more than all other sciences; the arts of legislation and administration and negotiation ought to take the place of, indeed exclude, in a manner, all other arts. I must study politics and war, that our sons may have liberty to study mathematics and philosophy. Our sons ought to study mathematics and philosophy, geography, natural history and naval architecture, navigation, commerce and agriculture in order to give their children a right to study painting, poetry, music, architecture, statuary, tapestry and porcelain.

We too must have a plan of progression. If not we are doomed, for without a vision the people will perish – not may perish but will perish.

What are we passing on to the next generation? What are we leaving as their inheritance? Be assured, what we show them today they will employ tomorrow.

Jesus believed that we would believe on him after he gave his life. He took the beating, abuse, and suffering because he loved us. This was a very necessary and risky investment in humanity on God's behalf. In like manner we must love our young boys to manhood. We must let them know that they are awesome individuals who need a savior. Because of Jesus' unselfish act of going to meet the cross untold numbers have come to Christ and received him as their savior. We must have just as much passion about our young men coming into their maturity and we must provide clear models of the ideal person we expect them to be. We must believe in them as individuals without being condescending or apathetic to their contribution to the greater community.

We adults must invest in our boys. We must use the Bible, the Word of God, as our moral conductor. We must bring our boys to our loving Father who saves us from ourselves. We must have a vision, and with this vision we will not perish.

# Contributors

*The Reverend Kip Bernard Banks, Sr.* serves as the Senior Pastor of the East Washington Heights Baptist Church of Washington, DC where he is working to build-up an intergenerational family of disciples who love God, love neighbors and transform the community with the Gospel of Jesus Christ. Among his many public and civic involvements, Rev. Banks has served as a senior aide to the US Senate Budget Committee and the Interim General Secretary of the Progressive National Baptist Convention, Inc.

*The Reverend Kenneth D.R. Clayton* is the Senior Pastor of the St. Luke Baptist church of Paterson, NJ where he has served since 1997. A graduate of New York Theological Seminary (M.Div.), he is a past Moderator of the Shiloh Baptist Association of NJ and President of the United Baptist Convention of NJ. He currently serves as Statistician of the National Baptist Convention, USA, Inc. He is the proud father of twin sons Kenneth and Kendrick.

*The Reverend Melvin Cotton, Jr.* is the Pastor of New Genesis Baptist Church. He holds a B.A. in Religion from Liberty University, and a M.A. and M.Div. from the School of Theology at Virginia Union University. He is married to Lakeesha Cotton with four children Yazmine, Melvin, Keyana and Caleb. He is a member of the Omega Psi Phi Fraternity, Inc.

*The Reverend John E. Guns* is Senior Pastor of the St Paul Church, Jacksonville, Florida. He is a deeply committed man to his family, his church and his community. As the founder of *Operation Save Our Sons*, Bishop Guns is very focused on working with men particularly young men. His goal is to see them mature to live healthy, godly lives, embodying the standard of Jesus Christ.

*The Reverend Dr. Harold Hudson* has served as senior pastor at Calvary Tremont Missionary Baptist Church in Columbus Ohio for the past 19 years. Previously, he swerved New Hope Baptist Church in Hillsboro Ohio for 10 years. He is the Vice President for African American and Multi-cultural Church Relations at United Theological Seminary in Dayton, Ohio, where he is also the Associate Dean of Doctoral Studies. He is married to Billie Sue Hudson and together they have seven children, seven grandchildren and seven great-grandchildren.

*The Reverend Tyrone P. Jones IV* is the Pastor of the historic First Baptist Church of Guilford, Columbia, MD, since 2011. Pastor Jones has been preaching the gospel for 20 years, and has served as a pastor for 14 years. Pastor Jones hails from Augusta, GA. He holds an M.Div. from Howard University and a

Th.M. from Princeton Seminary. He is currently a D.Min. candidate at Colgate Rochester Crozer Divinity School.

*The Reverend Dr. Lester Agyei McCorn* is the Senior Pastor of the historic Pennsylvania Avenue A.M.E. Zion Church in Baltimore. He is a faculty mentor of the Gardner C. Taylor Doctoral Fellows of United Theological Seminary. He is an inductee of the Martin Luther King Board of Preachers at his alma mater, Morehouse College. He is the author of *Standing on Holy Common Ground: An Africentric Ministry Approach to Prophetic Community Engagement*.

*The Reverend Attorney Aaron J. McLeod* is the Executive Director of Special Projects in the Office of the Senior Pastor at Trinity United Church of Christ in Chicago, Illinois. Rev. McLeod earned a J.D. from the University of Iowa College of Law, a M.Div. from Harvard University's School of Divinity, a B.A. in Business Administration with a concentration in Marketing from Morehouse College in Atlanta, GA, and he completed further studies at University of Illinois School of Public Health, Northwestern University, and Lancaster University in England. Rev. McLeod is married to Deidre Booker McLeod, and they are the proud parents of Thompson Brewer McLeod.

*The Reverend Dr. Wallace Murray* is the Assistant Pastor of the Trinity Christian Fellowship Center in Sarasota, Florida. Dr. Murray has been in ministry for over 40 years, traveling the U.S., Europe, East, West and South Africa, Asia, and the Caribbean with a focus on social, faith-based and justice initiatives. Dr. Murray holds a B.S. in Biblical Psychology and a Ph.D. in Divinity from TRICOMA College in Nigeria. He has attended FAMU, New College Florida's Honor College. Dr. Murray was Commissioner, Sarasota Housing Authority, is a member of NAR and FAR as a Realtor. The youngest of 18 children, he is married with 3 sons.

*The Reverend Dr. Keith A. Ogden* is the Senior Pastor of the Historic Hill Street Baptist Church in Asheville, NC. He's retired from the U.S. Army and is married to the former Patricia A. Craig for 28 years and with this union, they have a daughter, Taneshia Nicole, and 2 grandchildren, Tayshon and Ka'Lia.

*The Reverend Dr. James C. Perkins* has served as pastor of Greater Christ Baptist Church in Detroit, Michigan for thirty-three years. He currently serves as the President of The Progressive Baptist Convention, Inc. He is the author of *Building Up Zion's Walls: Ministry for Empowering the African American Family* and *Playbook for Christian Manhood: 12 Key Plays for Black Teen Boys*, published by Judson Press. Responding to the crisis he witnessed in the available educational options for young, urban African American males, Dr. Perkins instituted the Benjamin E. Mays Male Academy in 1993. This kindergarten through sixth grade Christian school for boys operated for 17 years and positively impacted the future of hundreds of males. Dr. Perkins is married to Linda Adkins Perkins and is the father of two daughters and the grandfather of one grandson.

*The Reverend Timothy Mark Rainey II* accepted his call to the ministry at the age of 16, majoring in Religion at Morehouse College in Atlanta, GA. Upon graduation, he enrolled in the Master of Divinity program at Princeton Theological Seminary in Princeton, NJ. Rev. Rainey has served at the historic Bright Hope Baptist Church in Philadelphia, PA. In 2009, he became the first Assistant Pastor of Indian Creek Church in Huntsville, AL, where he serves with his father, Elder Timothy Rainey. He is currently a Ph.D. student in Emory University's Graduate Division of Religion with a focus on American Religious Cultures. Married to Mrs. Brandi Burton Rainey, they are blessed with an energetic daughter, Jaci Elisabeth and a lively son, Timothy Mark III.

*The Reverend Daniel Corrie Shull* is the Senior Pastor of the Burnett Avenue Baptist Church in Louisville, Kentucky – a congregation committed to creating compelling environments in which people are developed into totally committed Disciples of Christ. In addition to preaching four times per weekend and providing leadership to a thriving congregation, Pastor Shull serves on a number of Boards for community organizations and institutions of higher education and also mentors youth. Additionally, he holds degrees from Fisk University and Louisville Presbyterian Theological Seminary and works as an adjunct professor for Louisville area colleges. In May of 2009, he was married to Abby Norman, and they are the parents of one son, Daniel Harrison.

*The Reverend Darryl Sims* is the proud father of three daughters, Darnisha Sims, Latecia Sims-Mix, and Riele Sims. He is the editor of numerous books of sermons by prominent Black ministers. *Sound the Trumpet: Messages to Empower African American Males*, (Judson Press, 2003) and its sequel, *Sound the Trumpet, Again* (2005). Along with *These Sisters Can Say It* (MMGI Books, 2009. 2014), *The Burden Bearer* (MMGI Books, 2011) and *Evangelizing and Empowering the Black Male*, (2013). He has authored *Adam Come Home: Liberating the Minds of Black Men* (MMGI Books, 2013). Reverend Sims has become nationally recognized as a conduit for providing spiritual and social renewal for Black men. He has provided workshops around the country to empower and heal Black men. He has also worked with a variety of schools and organizations in the areas of conflict resolution, academic achievement, and enhancement of racial pride.

*The Reverend Dr. Leonard N. Smith* has served as the Senior Minister of the Mount Zion Baptist Church in Arlington, Virginia for nearly 25 years. Additionally, he is the Chancellor of Richmond Virginia Seminary, Richmond, Virginia, and the Global Leader of Pastors in Global United Fellowship. A highly sought after leader, lecturer, preacher, teacher and the author of *We Need To Talk: Saying What We Have To Say Without Hurting Each Other*.

*The Reverend Dr. Raynard D. Smith* i;b end (Ph.D., Psychology and Religion, Drew University) is Associate Professor of Pastoral Care/Pastoral Theology at New Brunswick Theological Seminary in New Brunswick, NJ. An ordained elder in the Church of God in Christ, he is the Coordinator of the COGIC Scholars Fellowship, editor of the COGIC Scholars newsletter, The Advocate, and a member of the COGIC Board of Education. He is the author of a forthcoming publication Come Sunday Morning: Black Churches as Healing Communities.

*Bishop Derek T. Triplett i*s a respected preacher, pastor, radio and television personality, and relationship coach. He is the author of When I Became a Man: A Perspective on Manhood, Life and Relationships and a frequent guest speaker in seminars and conferences in churches, schools, colleges and universities. He is also founder of Getting All Males Equipped (G.A.M.E.), a mentoring group for youth and young adult males. He lives in Daytona Beach, Florida

*Bishop Hezekiah Walker* is the visionary, founder and Senior Pastor of the Love Fellowship Tabernacle Churches in Brooklyn, New York and Bensalem, Pennsylvania. Pastor Walker shepherds a growing and multi-cultural flock of members varying in age, race and socio-economic backgrounds. Born and raised in Brooklyn in the tumultuous Fort Greene public housing projects, he has risen to build and lead one of the greatest ministries in the Northeast.

# Adam Come Home

## LIBERATING THE MINDS OF BLACK MEN

# DARRYL D. SIMS

FOREWORD BY CAIN HOPE FELDER

# Other Books by MMGI Books

*A Charge to Keep* by Tokunbo Adelekan

*Adam Come Home* by Darryl D. Sims

*Evangelizing and Empowering the Black Male*

*Insanity of Theology* by G. Martin Young

*Just Preach: Primitive Baptist Style*

*Navigating Pastoral Leadership in the Transition Zone* by D. Darrell Griffin

*Standing on Holy Common Ground* by Lester A. McCorn

*Stronger in My Broken Places* by Charles E. Booth

*The Burden Bearer*

*The Gospel According to Cancer* by Patricia Gould-Champ

*These Sisters Can Say It*

*These Sisters Can Say It, Volume 2*